I0683417

Manifesting Mastery

FROM NOTHING ⟋ EVERYTHING

LOVE+
TRUTH | dōjō

Dedication

This course and workbook are dedicated to you—just for being willing to be a Student of Life itself you are already a visionary, high achiever, leader, A-player, innovator, change agent, and change maker,

To learn, grow, expand, evolve, and rise up into our fullest potential and most authentic expression of our own unique genius we must first be humble enough to embrace that there are areas we have not yet gained full mastery. This is in fact an act of grace and self-love as by having the courage to admit this to ourselves, we open the door the new worlds for us to experience as a lived experience.

All new worlds we wish to bring into our life as a lived experience—no matter what that might be—are like a house we recognize in the form of a desire. We then must go find the door to get into this house, and once we find the door we must discover the key that will unlock the door so we may step into the house and take ownership of it.

This course—done and completed in earnest—was created to grant you the key to whichever house you desire. I cannot help you choose which house to desire, but I can share the doors are always the same and there's a universal key that opens all of them.

My commitment and promise to you is to teach and guide you—to the best of my ability—how to discover, master, embody, and become this universal key that unlocks all doors to the dreams and desires within you.

The Powers already within you are your key. They might need to be aroused and awakened—that's what this course is all about—but please know that you are the universal key that unlocks the doors to your Heaven on Earth.

All I ask of you is to do your part—show up fully for the coursework ahead—and I will reveal and guide you to all what I described above.

I see you and the view is magnificent.

Love+Truth,

Robert

To discover and realize that everything material (aka "manifest") originates in that which we refer to as "nothing" (aka "ether" or "unmanifest") is to start to know that manifestation mastery is truly all about the alchemy of how the unmanifest becomes manifest.

This book and course was designed to demystify this alchemical process which is all about inner transformations that are in harmonious accord with a higher Octave of awareness, wisdom and Being.

Consciousness has two states: the formless unmanifest and manifest form

Everything manifest has its origins in the unmanifest

FROM NOTHING ⌇ EVERYTHING

LOVE+TRUTH | dōjō

This book is complimented by a Manifesting Mastery online course available in Robert Althuis' private teaching portal he refers to as the **"Love+Truth Dojo."**

For more information, click the QR code below or visit:

www.robertalthuis.com

Table of Contents

Course Instructions

Course Outline.. 2

Course Structure.. 6

Course Intentions.. 10

Self-Study

Manifestation 101.. 20

Lesson Chapters - Qualities of Being

01 - Ownership... 76

02 - Clarity... 88

03 - Commitment... 100

04 - Integrity.. 112

05 - Discipline.. 124

06 - Concentration... 136

07 - Fortitude... 148

08 - Resilience.. 160

09 - Mastery... 172

10 - Completion.. 184

11 - Shoshin... 196

12 - Gratitude... 208

Bonus - Temperance.. 220

Author's Bio

About Robert... 232

"NO MAN IS FREE WHO IS NOT A MASTER OF HIMSELF."

Course Outline

LOVE+
TRUTH™

Course Outline

-01-
OWNERSHIP
The journey from VICTIMHOOD to ACCOUNTABILITY

-02-
CLARITY
The journey from DISORDER to DISCERNMENT

-03-
COMMITMENT
The journey from INDECISION to TENACITY

-04-
INTEGRITY
The journey from DECEIT to HONOR

-05-
DISCIPLINE
The journey from SLOTH to VIGOR

-06-
CONCENTRATION
The journey from DISORGANIZATION to FOCUS

-07-
FORTITUDE
The journey from SOFTNESS to GRIT

LOVE+ TRUTH. | dōjō

RESILIENCE

The journey from FRAGILITY to AGILITY

MASTERY

The journey from INCOMPETENCE to GENIUS

COMPLETION

The journey from DEFEATISM to ENDURANCE

SHOSHIN

The journey from FALSE PRIDE to RECEPTIVENESS

GRATITUDE

The journey from MOROSITY to VISION

TEMPERANCE

The journey from GLUTTONY to MAGNANIMITY

"A BOAT IS SAFE IN HARBOR, BUT THAT IS NOT THE PURPOSE OF THE BOAT."

- Paolo Coelho -

Course Structure

LOVE+
TRUTH™

"WITHOUT ACTION, YOU AREN'T GOING ANYWHERE."

- Mahatma Gandhi -

COURSE STRUCTURE

There's an intentional design and structure to this course to maximize the potential benefit to you in the most efficient way possible. My aim in creating this course is to have it materially change your Life in tangible and meaningful ways. In addition, I realize your time is precious as we each have many demands on us no matter where we are in Life so efficiency was big factor as well.

Below is my recommended way to engage with this course; and, at the same time we each learn in different ways so if you wish to do it in another way than by all means do it the way that works best for you. The point though is to truly do this whole course and do it well as half-ass inputs begets half-ass outputs.

- INSTRUCTIONS -

Pre-Work
There's an exercise to set your intentions and a "Manifestation 101" self-study part to this course—ideally, you complete these before jumping into the chapters.

The Chapters & Classes
There will be a live 2-hour class on each chapter—the first c. 45 min will be a teaching on the chapter, then there will a short break (~5 min or so) followed by Q&A open discussion. If you miss a live session or are enrolled in the online course, there will be a recording of the class available in your online student portal.

Ideally, in preparation for each class, you read just the Teaching in that chapter. The exercises are to be done after the class.

Group Support
Once you sign up for the course, you will be invited to a private group for this course where you can interact with other course participants, pose questions, share experiences, etc.

Course Intentions

LOVE+
TRUTH

"IF YOU WANT TO CHANGE THE FUTURE, YOU MUST CHANGE WHAT YOU DO IN THE PRESENT."

- Mark Twain -

MY INTENTIONS

Your intentions for this course are not just some lofty and dreamy aspirations for the things and experiences you'd like to "call" into your Life. This course is not about calling in anything, it's about creating it as we move from wishing, hoping, and praying to stepping into the embodiment of Being "that" which is in resonance with "what" we want to experience in and as our Life.

These intentions then are ironclad promises we make to ourselves. And, in this promise we capture "that" which we desire to create in our Life and then we immediately let go of the eventual outcome or result. As soon as we have defined the promise, we hold that in our vision but we immediately shift all our energy into becoming - Being - "that" which is in resonance with our promise.

We follow and trust this process because we know and accept that we don't control outcomes and results, we only control the inputs which is solely in the domain of who we are Being. Becoming then is merely the journey of embodying the Being which is in sympathetic resonance with "that" which we want to create and experience in our Life.

This entire Universe is a perfect design created by an infinite intelligence and it operates in perfect Order in infinitely intelligent ways. Manifestation and all of Creation is governed by operation of immutable Cosmic Laws; there are no such things as luck, flukes, accidents, coincidences, or random events.

Everything is always in perfect Order, it simply cannot be any other way. The only reason we perceive things as out of Order is because we don't understand these Cosmic Laws, the manifestation process, or we can't see - let alone comprehend - all the billions of variables at play at any given moment.

We must learn to trust the process so we can focus our energy solely on "that" part which we control which is who we are Being. But, there's no way to truly trust anything we don't know or understand so in the next Chapter - Manifestation 101 - we're going explore how Manifestation truly works so we create the foundational understanding necessary to move into trusting the process.

But, first, let's set our intentions on the next page.

EXERCISE

Take some time (5-10 min) to contemplate your intentions for your Life. What do you want to create or experience in your Life? This is not an essay question, aim to be brief and specific and don't allow any limiting beliefs to hold you back. These intentions may be small or big, shallow or deep, superficial or profound, carnal or spiritual, it doesn't matter except they must be truthfully what you aspire to create or experience in Life. The Universe doesn't judge what you desire; hence, there's no right or wrong intention. It merely operates by Cosmic Law, and if your Being is in sympathetic resonance with "that" which you wish to create or experience than "that" will manifest in some form or shape.

- INSTRUCTIONS -

Intention #1

Your intention should be brief, specific, and truthful. Absolute clarity is key here, not whether you think or believe it's possible or realistic for you.

My Why

Here you can get a little more poetic and fuzzy, what we're after is your "why" which is always something you expect to "gain" from what you desire.

Hint: your deepest "why" is typically something you expect to "feel" like once you realize your intention.

Notes

Leave this open for now, later in the Course we're going to revisit these intentions and we'll use the Notes section to revisit the original intentions and your why.

Note: Set at least one intention for this Course, but you may set up to five as you wish.

Intention

My Why

Notes

Intention

_____
_____
_____

My Why

_____
_____
_____
_____
_____
_____
_____
_____
_____

Notes

_____
_____
_____
_____
_____
_____
_____
_____
_____

Intention

_____

_____

_____

My Why

_____

_____

_____

_____

_____

_____

_____

_____

Notes

_____

_____

_____

_____

_____

_____

_____

_____

Intention

My Why

Notes

LOVE+ TRUTH. | dōjō

Intention

My Why

Notes

Manifestation 101

LOVE+
TRUTH

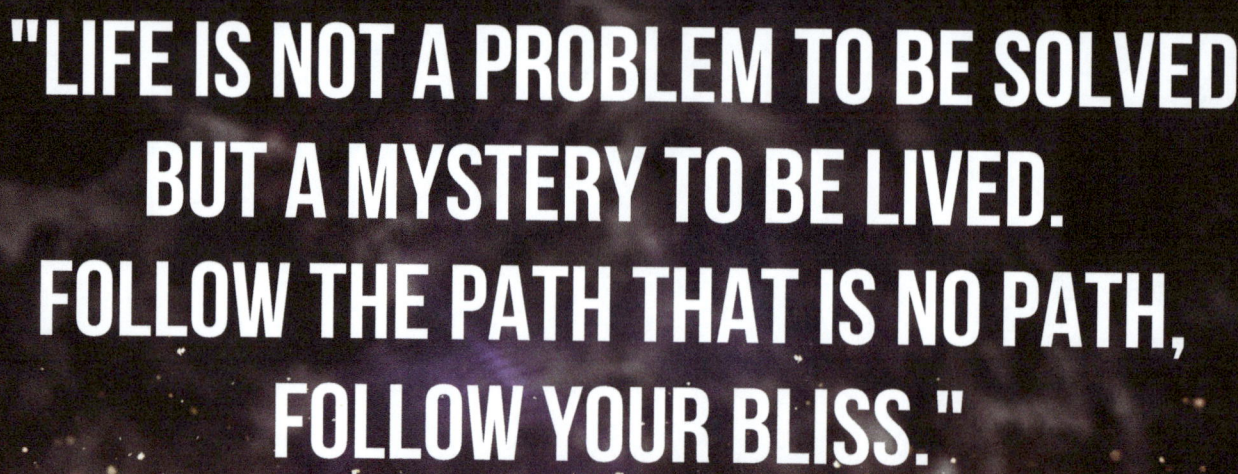

"LIFE IS NOT A PROBLEM TO BE SOLVED
BUT A MYSTERY TO BE LIVED.
FOLLOW THE PATH THAT IS NO PATH,
FOLLOW YOUR BLISS."

- Joseph Campbell -

SELF-STUDY

No Woo Woo.

This course is not The Secret revisited, nor will it provide fluffy promises of vast and easy richesby simply "vibing" at the right frequency.

This is not one of the many manifestation courses that are created and taught by people who have never created anything expect a successful coaching business, where your tuition pays for their lifestyle. This is not a course that will try to sell you superhuman manifestation codes that you can only access through me.

The Truth is, there are no secret codes. There is no amount of meditation, breathwork, mantras, visualization, special incense, or vision-boarding that will automatically manifest anything for you in the material world. These are all beautiful practices, so don't abandon them. But manifestation works through and by operation of Cosmic laws,and in this chapter, I am going to pick apart the process and demystify how your ideas, dreams, aspirations, and desires—all

of which live in the unmanifest mental and spiritual realm—can be actualized - i.e. manifested - into the manifest material world we experience as our reality.

No codes, no gimmicks, no woo woo stuff that's entirely intangible and often inactionable. I will share only what's tangible and can be directly acted on. I'll explain why and how it works in plain and simple terms so you can understand the science and mechanics woven into the very art of manifestation.

About Frequency & Vibration.

One of the most popular manifestation teachings goes as follows: if you can only access the frequency and vibration of financial abundance, the perfect love relationship, or that new house you always wanted, you will spontaneously and effortlessly manifest it into your reality.

While some of this is tried-and-true, it's vastly incomplete and all practical utility is lost in this over-simplification of how the unmanifest is made manifestas an experience of our reality.

For example, take the manifestation coaches that offer these teachings. What actually manifested the material success they use as advertising for their prowess in manifesting? I promise you it wasn't just their meditation practices or visualization techniques. They didn't miraculously tune into the right frequency and vibration and then all sorts of material success flooded their way.

No, what "manifested" their material success was being very savvy at social media, writing ad copy, and marketing their services.They gained a certain level of mastery in how to create courses, workshops, events, and then they mastered how to package it all together. All of this is admirable and I applaud their success whole-heartedly—but, to keep it real, we must speak Truth and not fairytales.

What's real is that anyone who's successfully manifested anything in the material realm—whether it be wealth, health, love, or anything else—did so by first becoming "that" which is in sympathetic resonance with "that" which they manifested.

I recommend you read that sentence again because it's important to internalize. Don't worry about knowing what sympathetic resonance means yet,

worry about knowing what sympathic resonance really is as we'll do a deep dive on that shortly.

When we speak of becoming "that," we're pointing at embodiment or who we are Being.

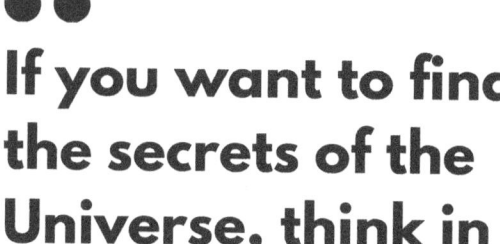

If you want to find the secrets of the Universe, think in terms of energy, frequency and vibration.

- Nikola Tesla -

The quality of who we are Being has a certain frequency and vibration, which most of you reading this probably understand very well.

If our Being has the quality of being depressed and down,that has a certain frequency and vibration.

Similarly, if our Being has the quality of being joyful and optimistic, that also has a distinct energy "thumbprint." All energy resonates at a certain frequency which translates into vibration.

In fact, everything resonates at a certain frequency and vibration;

22

think about groups, parties, concerts, mass protests, or even buildings, cities, or countries. Nature "vibrates" at a distinctly different frequencyfrom a busy city. Moreover, cities, states, countries, all places in general really have their own distinct "vibe" as, for example, New York City feels very different from Paris and so forth.

Frequency is largely inaudible to the human ear and intangible to our senses. We resonate with vibrations and frequencies in a way that often transcends our physical senses. We all "feel" and "sense" energy and the texture of energy is its vibration and frequency.

Although there is a scientific nuance as the harmonic phenomenon we call frequencies, which we measure in sinusoidal waves (or "sin waves"), are technically a derivative of vibrations. Or, in other words, frequencies are the effect of the cause called vibrations or, in yet other words, when some "thing" vibrates this produces a frequency. Clearly, this topic goes much deeper but for this course this is not important so when I use either term I am pointing at the same thing.

Before we move on and dive into the underlying science and mechanics of manifestation, first we must close out this topic of Being. This will clarify where this course is

a fairly radical departure from other manifestation teachings.

Here's the crux of it: you cannot directly influence, affect, change, or tune your frequency and vibration unless you're at extraordinarily high levels of human consciousness. I am talking sage level and above, a level 99%+ of us are simply not at—and that includes yours truly.

So, how do us mortals change and tune our frequency and vibration?

The answer is very simple: by who we are Being. Who we are Being has a distinct vibrational thumbprint, and while we can act on who we are Being, we cannot reverse engineer who we are Being through miraculously tuning into the frequency and vibration that's a product or derivative of that very Being.

You see, Being is the cause and frequency and vibration are the effect. You cannot change any cause by working on the level of effect. This is elementary science, not opinion.

In fact, even the sage follows this science, except the sage is so masterful tuning into his/her Being that it appears as if they are able to effortlessly and instantaneously dial into a certain frequency and vibration.

To round out the topic of Being, let's explore what actually creates or makes up our present moment "Beingness."

Again, this is also very simple, our total Beingness in the present moment is the amalgamation of all qualities of Being that we are being in that very moment.

Ok, fair enough, but what then are qualities of Being?

We all know qualities of Being because they're all the qualities we can embody and express. Joy, happiness, courage, calm, confidence, compassion are beautiful qualities of Being, and there are countless more.

Conversely, there are also qualities of Being which we experience as a gradient of suffering such as stress, anxiety, overwhelm, anger, worry, boredom, and unworthiness (and again there are countless more).

This whole course - when we get into the meat of it - is centered around twelve qualities of Being that I have discovered in my own life as manifestation superpowers.

These are not the only ones by any means, but embodying these twelve will inject rocket fuel into anyone's manifestation capabilities regardless of what we want to manifest.

These are all qualities that we can act on. They are not tricks and gimmicks; they are simple and tangible qualities that we can work towards mastering.

I know that doesn't sound very sexy, and I am not going to bamboozle you and tell you all of this is easy or takes no effort on your part. It does and will. At first, it will stretch and challenge you, and there will be some uneasy moments where you will want to toss the towel into the ring.

That's all part of the natural process of growth, transformation, and expansion. If we want our future to change, we must first change within. Our Outer World is a holographic reflection of our Inner World. Change your Inner World - i.e who you are Being - and your Outer World will inevitably change by operationof Cosmic laws.

Incidentally, this is why all this also works for people who do "bad" things. The Universe harmonizes all of Creation through the immutable law of Karma and all Karmic debts will eventually have to be repaid; hence, it doesn't judge, condemn, or block certain manifestations over others.

Basically, manifestation itself – that which is "created" - occurs by operation of Cosmic laws which are neutral to the "means" used or the

LOVE+ TRUTH | dōjō

"intent" behind the manifestation. However, the Manifestor (i.e. Creator) is responsible and accountable for all its manifestations (i.e. creations) through the immutable law of Karma.

This explains how Pablo Escobar could accumulate unfathomable riches—I promise you he didn't get there via meditation or vision boarding. Instead, he embodied certain qualities of Being which he then chose to express in creating a global drug-trafficking enterprise until the law caught up with him.

For Pablo to manifest the financial riches he did, he must have believed this was a potentiality that was possible for him. He then acted on this belief in all the ways he did to translate this unmanifest thought-form into a manifest lived experience on the material plane.

With this foundational knowledge in place, it's time to transition into the scientific mechanics of all of Creation. Manifestation is merely a subpart of all of Creation along with —in broad terms—existence and de-manifestation. This is of course the cycle of Life itself which we can see and witness on all levels within our Universe.

This cycle of Life is readily observable for us with biological life forms but, for instance, even our

our own Sun was created some 4.6 billion years ago and is estimated to be in existence for another 5 billion years when it will run out of hydrogen and dissolve which is the process of de-manifestation.

Everything in our Universe follows this universal cycle of Life where we, in scientific terms, refer to the inevitable decline and eventual death of a "thing" (whatever that "thing" might be) as the process of entropy which has its foundation in the second law of thermodynamics.

Power of the Mind, Psycho-Cybernetics & Neuroscience.

We're now going to explore the science and mechanics behind the process of manifestation from two distinct vantage points, which we could describe as the mechanics of our Inner World and the mechanics of the Outer World. The fusion and interaction between these two interrelated and interdependent forces is what creates our manifest reality.

I will cover the basics, or what you would expect in a 101-level course. We're not after a PhD; rather, the objective is to offer you a practical field guide that's actionable and can help you gain mastery and enhanced results in manifesting "that" which you desire and wish to experience in your Life.

Also, there's no test and you don't even have to understand or believe in any of it for it to work. The immutable Cosmic laws that govern this entire Universe are indifferent whether you agree with them or not.

The reason to want to understand them, and better yet believe in them, is because it's nearly impossible to trust "that" which we simply don't know or understand.

If we can't trust it, we can have no faith in that it will work for us.

Without this faith and trust, we're stacking the deck against ourselves to do what is required to shift into the level of Being commensurate in frequency and vibration of "that" which we wish to manifest as an experience in our Life or reality.

The only person you're destined to become is the person you decide to be.

- Ralph Waldo Emerson -

Hence, perhaps the most important reason to internalize the science and mechanics of manifestation to gain faith and trust that it works by knowing how it works.

So, here we must go a little into some nerdy science territory, but don't worry, we only need to know the basics.

First, we have to embrace the fact that nothing is fixed or static in this Universe and that includes human beings. Everything is always changing and evolving; everything is in constant motion as this Universe and everything within it grows, expands, and evolves in the eternal process of evolution. In the wise words of the brilliant Stoic philosopher Heraclitus:

Nothing ever is, everything is in the process of becoming.

And so too are you and I. From the moment of our first breaths until our very last, we're always and forever becoming. Even when we don't think we are, we're growing, evolving, and expanding—and this makes sense because we are all just a personified fractal of this entire Universe.

From advances in the science of epigenetics, we now even know that our DNA is not fixed, and the expression of our DNA is estimated to be 95%+ malleable. This means that our DNA predetermines only 5% of our physical expression

expression including our health or any genetic ailments or diseases.

We have known much longer through the advances in neuroscience that our Mind is even more malleable through the phenomenon of neuroplasticity.

Our Minds are basically like hard drives with software installed, and this software can be edited, updated, expanded, and deleted. We also know that if we have limiting beliefs, these act like "malware" and stifle our ability to manifest that which we (falsely) believe is not available to us.

In this very moment, should you be thinking that all this is not true for you, that would in fact be a limiting belief which then makes this not available to you. Not because it's not true or doesn't work, but your very belief it doesn't work for you creates the self-fulfilling prophecy which proves this (false) limiting belief to you.

We're going to go deeper into limiting beliefs when we explore the psycho-cybernetic loop, which comes up next in the next section.

But, before we do so, there's one thing of parament importance I want you to take away from all of this:

We don't really need to know or understand our limiting beliefs, we can overwrite them simply by creating new empowering beliefs.

I'll show you why this is true and how to do this before this chapter is over, so let's now do a deep dive in what's called the psycho-cybernetic loop, which is a fancy term for how our human operating system functions and creates our reality.

The psycho-cybernetic Loop shows us in simple terms how our Mind works. Our Mind is the ethereal realm of thoughts, ideas, imaginations, and memories whereas our brain is the physical organ in our body.

Another way to conceptualize this is our brain is the hardware, and our Mind is the software.

As you read the explanation of the psycho-cybernetic loop that follows, please refer to the graphic illustration of the psycho-cybernetic loop on the next page and reference it as often as you need, as sometimes a picture can tell a thousand words.

Let's start at the point of origin which is labeled the Egoic Mind. The moment we're born, our Mind (most notably the subconscious mind) starts collecting data through our five senses (i.e., eyes, ears, ears, mouth, and skin or touch).

Technically, this starts when we're in the womb, but to keep it simple, let's work with the starting point as when we take our very first breath.

From this moment onwards, our subconscious mind starts accumulating, interpreting, and storing all the information that's

meaning our conscious mind derives from it, is what colors (or fogs over) the lens through which we see, experience, and interpret the entire world or reality around us and Life itself.

The miraculous thing to understand about the subconscious mind is that it has virtually unlimited storage capacity and incredible processing speed. It's able to take in

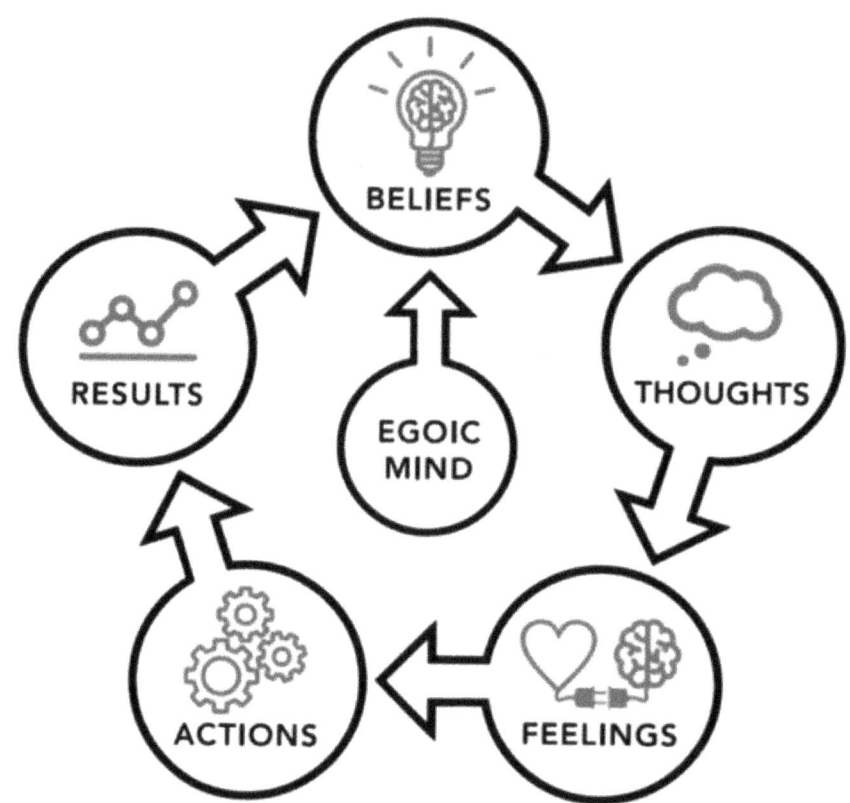

flooding in through our five senses to start building a vast database of our experiences.

This remarkable human super-computer database of all our experiences will serve the rest of our lives as the central reference point for how we perceive the world. This database, and the

severything—and I mean every single granular bit of data that floods in through our five senses. Our conscious mind can only process approximately 10% of all the data that floods in through our five senses, but our subconscious mind captures the full 100% without any conscious effort or control on our part.

LOVE+ TRUTH | dōjō

The part of our Mind that determines which 10% is filtered out to be registered by our conscious mind, and what simply passes through unconsciously is called the Reticular Activating System, or RAS. More on this later as we delve deeper into the inner workings of the psycho-cybernetic loop and how we can use this to our advantage.

When we are around three years old, our conscious mind comes fully online. The moment this happens is the moment we develop a sense of self and others. We become aware of our persona or personal self as distinct and separate from others and the world we live in, and this is why we refer to this moment as the origin point of our Egoic Mind.

From this moment forward, we will be experiencing and perceiving ourselves Life itself, and our entire reality through the "eyes" of our Egoic Mind.

This ego (or self or persona) is a fictional character that is entirely created, animated, and perpetuated by the Egoic Mind.

From this moment forward, we will be experiencing and perceiving ourselves Lifeitself, and our entire reality through the "eyes" of our Egoic Mind.

This ego (or self or persona) is a fictional character that is entirely created, animated, and perpetuated by the Egoic Mind.

Yes, the small self or Ego is merely an idea, a psychological construct, which means it's simply not real.

The only "thing" that's truly real is "that" which observes our thoughts, as we are not our thoughts just as we are not our body. We have thoughts and we have a body, but "some thing" is aware of all of this. We can refer to this as the Observer, but if you prefer, we can also say this is our true Self or our Soul. In Vedic traditions, they refer to this as our Atman.

Words are just linguistic labels, and all these words point at the same thing, so it makes no difference which one you prefer to use.

What's key is the understanding which at all times is a remembrance, as we each already know everything there's is to know about everything. We're just on the journey of remembrance of who we truly are.

The moment it "clicks" inside of us that we'renot our thoughtsor our bodies, but the Observer who has thoughts and has a body—this is the moment we have started to awaken from the dream of life or

Life or what's referred to as "maya" in Vedic traditions.

Those who are awake all live in the same world, those who are asleep live in their own worlds.

- Heraclitus -

That initial grand awakening is not the thrust of this course, so I am not going to expand on it. What we're after in this Manifestation Mastery course is how to bridge the unmanifest spiritual realm of thoughts, ideas, dreams, aspirations, and imaginations (i.e. our Inner World) and anchor and actualize those in the manifest material realm (i.e. our Outer World) as a lived experience in our reality.

I would like to share one more key understanding, as nothing stuns spiritual growth and expansion more than a false sense of spiritual Ego. While crossing the threshold of this initial awakening representsa radical shift in our understanding of Life itself, this awakening is not the finish line. It's only the starting point of our journey of growth and expansion. We will each encounter

countless more profound awakenings, each time opening up a new grander, richer, and more beautiful dimension of a higher order.

Let's return to the discussion of our thoughts, which we just concluded are not real. Yet, it's undeniable that we do have thoughts as well as beliefs. The understanding we're after here is that they are psychological constructs, and in that sense, they are not real as in fixed, tangible, or unchangeable.

Our thoughts and beliefs are much like software as we discussed earlier. And, just like software, our thoughts and beliefs can be edited, upgraded, enhanced, and also deleted.

Moreover, software can be very powerful and enabling; at the same time, software can also be corrupted or infected with malware which disables the software.

Our limited beliefs are essentially malware, they impede our ability to actualize those experiences we desire to bring into our Life as a lived experience.

The paradoxical nature of beliefs is that they are simultaneously our greatest ally and our greatest adversary, depending on whether the belief is empowering or limiting.

The cause of this is because within any belief we have is the imbedded presumption and understanding that they are true. If this belief is empowering in nature, it will propel us forward and to new heights.

However, a limiting belief acts like an invisible glass ceiling as we falsely believe some "thing" is not possible, available, or accessible to us. Limiting beliefs come in all sorts of colors, and usually, but not always, we picked them up in our childhood. This makes them deeply entrenched and extraordinarily hard to pinpoint as—again—we simply believe they are true, and this is how we perceive the world.

So, beliefs are pesky little buggers that are hard to discover by ourselves. Moreover, they are very challenging to change directly. So, what do we do?

The good news is that we can very effectively overwrite them with empowering beliefs, and we can then rely on neuroscience and neuroplasticity to come to our aid.

You see, from neuroscience we unequivocally know that "neurons that fire together, wire together."

We also know that neurons that no longer fire together will over time no longer wire together, as the neural pathways dissolve when they go unused.

This means that we don't need to change or modify our limiting beliefs directly, we just need them to go unused and they will dissolve over time.

In fact, we don't even need to know them or their origins, so while we can go this route, we really don't need to revisit our childhood wounds and traumas to understand how, where, and why we adopted these limiting beliefs.

There's a much more simple and direct way, and I like simple and efficient over complicated and inefficient.

Having said that, there is a place and time where revisiting deep traumas can be powerful medicine and even necessary to evolve beyond the trauma or wound we have. This is especially the case when it involves opioid addictions, sexual and emotional abuse, or other gross violations of our human rights or human dignity.

This course is not designed for that sort of healing, but there are true miracle workers and qualified therapists that can guide you through the healing work and process that this sort of trauma work requires. I encourage you to seek their help if you feel your limiting beliefs stem from traumas of that nature.

To understand the simple way I prefer and advocate, we do need to gain one more pivotal understanding about beliefs. Each and every belief - whether empowering or limiting in nature - is at its very core a decision we made about ourselves or Life itself.

Maybe read that again as it's a biggie. Every belief we hold is a decision we made, and we can know this to be true because if you think about it, how else could this belief be true for us?

By definition, a belief is true to us because at some point—often in our childhood but this could be at any time in our past—we experienced something that we interpreted and

perceived in whatever way we did which then prompted us to make a decision about ourselves and/or Life itself.

The principle of Life is that Life responds to corresponding. Your Life becomes the thing you have decided it shall be.

- Raymond Charles Barker -

All experiences we have ever had occur to us in a certain way based on how we perceive them. Our subconscious mind automatically and autonomously interprets the experience based on referencing its vast database of other memorized experiences, and then creates a meaning or narrative of that experience. The moment it decides what this experience "means" about ourselves, or Life itself, the Mind has effectively created a belief about ourselves or Life itself which it then holds to be true.

"How" we perceive something and "what" meaning we assignto it is heavily biased by our upbringing, family traditions, schooling, societal norms and values, culture, faith-based teachings, and the entire outer world environment we live in.

Collectively, all of these become our encultured conditioning and the lens through which we perceive ourselves and the world around us.

At the very core of all our encultured conditioning—which are just beliefs we hold—is a decision we made about ourselves and Life itself, and these beliefs are entirely malleable. In other words, we can change, enhance, upgrade, delete, or overwrite them with beliefs that empower us.

LOVE+ TRUTH | dōjō

The question then becomes how we do we actually do that?

That, like all things of a divinely intelligent nature, is simple and elegant.

First, wherever we hold a limiting belief, whether we know or suspect it, we make a new decision about ourselves or Life itself.

Second, we start stacking evidence to support this new decision, which is solely to demonstrate to our vigilant Mind that it can let go of the old (limiting) belief and adopt the new empowering belief.

Our Mind will always gravitate toward what is familiar as it perceives the known to be comfortable and safe. The "unknown" is a quagmire because the Mind detests the unfamiliar and unknown, which moves it into discomfort and feeling unsafe. This is a protection mechanism hardwired into the Mind, it is neither good nor bad, it is just how our Mind is wired to respond.

Hence, this evidence is crucial as we need to feed our mind data that supports moving into the unfamiliar and unknown of this new belief which will empower us.

The highest quality data is that which we can collect from our own lived experiences. Often, this is

surprisingly easy when we direct our awareness (through the conscious mind) to go on a treasure hunt for evidence that supports the new empowering belief.

Turns out, we were literally blind to this evidence before because it got filtered out by our RAS, so it never registered in our conscious mind. Let's take a moment to explore how the RAS works in detail.

Assume a person had a limiting belief that he or she were terrible at "X." This was something they picked up in childhood because they did something and then their parents or teachers told them they were no good at "X" and would never be any good at it. They heard this repeatedly and started believing it, then they decided this must be true. As if guided by invisible hand, this became their lived reality as this belief expressed itself into their actual lived experiences.

However, there is most likely a lot of evidence in their life where this was not true at all. They were actually perfectly capable of "X," but this new evidence was never taken into consideration because their RAS filtered it out before it made it into their conscious awareness. The RAS was simply following the already-made decision that they were terrible at it.

This is what it means to consciously stack evidence based on retracing our own life experiences.

If something is possible for others, know it is possible for you also.

- Marcus Aurelius -

Second, if we can't find sufficient or any evidence in our own life experiences, we can look to the world around us and find evidence there.

Here's the spiritual principle that anchors this understanding: any Inner World capacity, power, or ability available to any person is available to all persons.

This means that, fundamentally, we are all wired the same way. One person's capacity or power to love, experience joy and happiness, or create success in their life is no different from anyone else's.

This is not to be confused with the notion we are all going to, or are meant to, experience the same Outer World experiences.

We're not all going to have Michael Jordan's success in basketball or become a billionaire in this lifetime.

But the Inner World capacities, powers, and abilities that Michael Jordan and the billionaire cultivated to realize their Outer World experience are readily available to any of us.

We're not designed to all have the same dreams and aspirations, and each of us have a unique life plan for this round of life in Earth School —and all of that is by perfectly intelligent design. Evolution thrives on diversity, not sameness and uniformity.

So, our experiences and results in the Outer World are never going to be identical and they don't need to be. In fact, it would be catastrophic on a multitude of levels if they were all identical.

True success from a Higher Order perspective is to live your unique life plan, realize your unique dreams and aspirations, and attain the self-realization you are an expression of Divinity in human form.

So, for all the "evidence" I provided above, you can know and trust that we can look for evidence in the world around us to stack evidence in support of the new empowering belief we decided on.

There's one more nuance I want to highlight, and I'll use an example to demonstrate this.

LOVE+ TRUTH | dōjō

Imagine someone with Stage 4 cancer and written off by conventional Western medicine.

For every incurable disease or condition, you can find an example (and often many) of what Western medicine can only explain as an inexplicable miraculous healing.

Since Western medicine and science can't explain it, they write it off as an anomaly. But, it's actually not an anomaly so much as it's a potentiality in the Universe that was actualized or made manifest.

For this healing to occur, an Inner World transformation took place which transmuted and cured the Stage 4 cancer as the body—and its health or disease—is part of our Outer World experience. At an energetic level, this Inner World transformation entailed a shift in vibration and frequency from one where the cancer could exist in the physical body to one where the cancer could no longer exist.

This isn't a medical course so I don't want to digress too much, but we can measure these frequencies and the natural resonant frequencies of virtually all diseases and those of health (homeostasis in medical terms) have been known for well over a century and as a medical modality is commonly referred to as frequency healing.

Everything is energy, match the frequency of the reality you want and you cannot help but get that reality. It can be no other way. This is not philosophy, this is physics.

- Bashar -

This salient quote by Bashar (as channeled by Darryl Anka) is often erroneously attributed to Albert Einstein, which makes sense when you consider Einstein's theory of relativity centers around the premise that matter and energy are in reality one and the same where matter is manifest energy and energy is unmanifest matter. We can extrapolate from this that all energy is a potentiality of unmanifest matter which can be made manifest.

Hence, if it's a potentiality in this Universe, then it's a possibility for any of us. We just need to come into sympathetic resonance with that potentiality and it will—

by operation of Cosmic law—alchemize into our manifest reality.

We've covered a lot of ground in a short amount time here as—again—this is a field guide more than a PhD in spiritual metaphysics. There are many great books written that can take you far deeper into this material—I even like to believe I wrote one of them—but in the interest of time, I am going to now circle back to the psycho-cybernetic loop as we're ready to truly grasp its simplicity and profundity. As I do, please refer to the previously graphic as often as you need to.

So far, we've covered the essence of the Egoic Mind and how it functions. We've also covered what beliefs are, how they form, and how we can overwrite them.

Next up in the psycho-cybernetic loop is our thoughts. Thoughts are also not real in that they are simply psychological constructs and therefore malleable and ever-changing. We all know this firsthand given that we have very different thoughts when we're happy or when we're sad or down.

According to the "brain facts" published by the Cleveland Clinic, the average person has anywhere from 60,000 to 80,000 thoughts every single day using 100 billion neurons that connect at more than

500 trillion points called synapses. We think thoughts incessantly and the vast majority (approx. 90-95% according to the National Science Foundation) of these thoughts are repetitive and autonomously generated by our subconscious mind. Whichever way you slice the pie, we think very little with our conscious mind relative to the copious thoughts produced by our subconscious mind.

The difference we're interested in is that we can consciously determine the quality of our thoughts when we produce them with our conscious mind; however, we have no control over the quality when they are produced by our subconscious mind.

Our subconscious mind is like a mindless (no pun intended) machine producing an endless stream of thoughts based on our imbedded beliefs which, as we explored earlier, are the decisions we made about ourselves or Life itself.

When these beliefs are empowering, it poses no problems—and it actually helps us. In this case, the subconscious mind will produce a steady current of empowering thoughts that help us propel toward what we desire to create as a lived experience. We call this the positive habituation of the Mind, or in plain English, we can speak of "positive mental habits."

Conversely, with limiting beliefs these habituated thought-patterns are blocking us from what we desire to create as a lived experience. So here the very same mechanics of the subconscious mind is harmingus much like a knife can be used to cut fresh fruit or harm another person.

This is why the quality of our deeply held subconscious beliefs are so pivotal in the moving towards our goals and aspirations for Life.

And, once again, we're faced with the maxim that if we want to change any effect, we must make changes at the level of the cause.

The cause of these thoughts produced by the subconscious mind is the beliefs it holds about ourselves and Life itself. Change those beliefs, and the thoughts will inevitably change accordingly. Then inevitably, our reality changes by operation of Cosmic law, which Bashar refers to as physics.

So far, so good and all true. But it is still not complete. Because the pscyho-cybernetic loop informs us there's much more in play for our reality to shift in meaningful ways.

This is because our prevailing thoughts dictate our emotions, so let's explore what that has to do with anything. As it turns out, our emotions have a lot to do with just about everything.

Our emotions (e.g., how we feel) are a direct product of our thoughts. Happy thoughts produce happy emotions, sad or depressing thoughts produce emotions which we experience as some form of suffering. It's that simple, and there's no exception or special rules.

The qualityof our thoughts dictate the quality of our emotions, or in other words, our emotionsare the effect of the cause called our thoughts.

The same maxim applies here: we cannot change the quality of our thoughts by workingon the level of effect (whichis our emotions). If you don't believe me, try suggesting to a deeply depressed person that all they need to do is change their emotions. Right, that will go nowhere.

So, while we cannot reverse-engineer our thoughts by changing our emotions, we can readily trace back the quality of our thoughts by feeling into our emotions. In many ways, our emotions are like the proverbial canary in the coalmine. They're impossible not to detect as they're highly visceral, and most importantly, they possess an extremely useful quality. You see, we can bullsh*t ourselves all day long with our thoughts, but there's no way to bullsh*t ourselves about our emotions.

When we feel happy, joyful, or confident, there's no mistake about it. Similarly, when we feel sad, ashamed, irritated, angry, overwhelmed, there's equally no mistake about it. Emotions get expressed not just ethereally; they lodge into our body, and we literally feel them in our gut.

Our Egoic Mind, on the other hand, can play all sort of tricks on us. It can easily get lost in its own stories and distortions of reality, which it then serves up as denials, excuses, justifications and all sorts of other righteousness which is really just mental drivel.

So, emotions are a much better compass of true North than our Mind is.

There's another pivotal role our emotions play. Our emotions, left unattended, have an outsized impact on our actions or inactions—or in other words, what we do and do not do.

The good news is that we can overwrite this with our conscious mind. We can be in deep suffering and feel like sh*t and still decide to

do or not do something anyway. This can only be done with the command of our conscious mind. Our subconscious mind only has one setting, and that is autopilot.

For us to do anything with and through our conscious mind, we must first be aware of it.

Awareness functions like the aperture of a camera. It can be virtually closed, which is the prevailing state of those at lower levels of consciousness. The aperture of our awareness then progressively opens as we rise in levels of consciousness, and we literally become more aware of a greater vista of Life itself. The level of Free Will available to us is directly correlated with the openness of our aperture of awareness. As our command of Free Will increases, our ability to create our own reality and dictate our destiny increases as well.

Mind you, with seeing and knowing more also comes a corresponding increase in accountability and responsibility for ourselves and the entire world around us.

So, Free Will is a double-edged sword. Be mindful of the powers you wish for as the Universe will bestow them on you in tandem with the duty to use and apply these powers in benevolent ways.

" Without action, you aren't going to go anywhere.

- Mahatma Gandhi -

Next up in the psycho-cybernetic loop is action. Here on the manifest material plane—Earth school if you will—the "language" that creates is action. We must do, act, or move the pieces on the chessboard for the game of life to come into motion for us.

Manifestation is the process of alchemizing "that" which lives and exists in the unmanifest spiritual realm into the manifest material realm. We won't meditate, breathwork, yoga, incense, or vision board ourselves to our earthly desires. Those can help and compliment bringing things to life within us, but there's no substitute for showing up for life.

Even if the Universe conspires in your favor—as it always does—you still need to show up. Even that perfect love partner that miraculously revealed him or herself still required you to show up in the same place, which presumably wasn't your living room. These are the rules and principles of the manifest material realm—we can fight against them or work with

them, but no amount of protest will do you any good. They apply equally to everything of creation within all of Creation.

Discrimination and special privileges are foreign concepts to the rules that govern the "game Spirit plays," whereas the "game Man plays" is admittedly littered with them. Yet, that still doesn't hold any of us back from anything as for every form of discrimination or special privileges one person claims blocks them from what they want and desire, there are countless examples of people that faced with similar facts and circumstances rose above and beyond them.

Hence, it's always possible, we just need to figure out how it can become a possibility for us.

Often, the most important "action" we can take is to work on and within our Inner World. This entire course is geared around cultivating and mastering the Inner World qualities of Being which will then inevitably shift our outer world experiences and reality.

This doesn't happen because you're now able to shape-shift your reality simply by magically dialing into the frequency and vibration of "that" which you desire to create as an experience in your Life. No, by cultivating and mastering these twelve qualities of Being, you will now—in a state of embodiment—do, act, and move anything which is required to co-create "that" which you desire as a lived experience.

It cannot be any other way; if you don't believe me, just put it to the test.

This allows us to close out the psycho-cybernetic loop. The final phase in this autonomous, self-propelled, and self-fulfilling prophecy manifestation process is results and outcomes.

Results and outcomes are what either reinforce our empowering or limiting beliefs, or they allow us to overwrite them even more powerfully if they are the product of new empowering beliefs we decided on.

Either way, the proof is always in the pudding. We cannot fake results and outcomes. We can lie and bamboozle ourselves about them, quit too soon to realize them, or never even really try, but the results and outcomes themselves don't lie. They are the hard facts and circumstances which make up our reality of lived experiences.

We can, and often do, misinterpret the results and outcomes. We can misread what they mean, why they came about or not about, and so forth. The reality is this: interpreting our results and

and outcomes in Life takes wisdom, and wisdom comes from experience. Experience comes from experimentation—literally—so the only way to "win" this game is by experimenting.

Inherent in experimenting often is failure; we're simply destined to inevitably experience failures and breakdowns when we experiment.

This is the nature of Life itself. Even Nature itself experiments all the time, and many things fail before they don't. We call that process evolution.

The key thing to internalize into the deepest corners of your psyche and Soul is that experiencing failures has no bearing on you being a failure.

In fact, as long as you're alive—however fragile or downtrodden that might be—you are a miraculous success.

That's right, just being alive is Being a wild success, everything else is bonus or extra sauce.

The trophies like fame, fortune, and applause the world tells you are important and a measure of your innate worth is a boldface lie of colossal proportions.

You are Divinity expressed into a human avatar, and unless you truly

40

believe God—or Creator, Source, Monad, Great Spirit, Most High, Oversoul, Brahman, Infinite Intelligence or whatever your preferred label might be—makes mistakes, then please take my wordsto heart that you cannot be a failure no matter how many failures you experience in your life.

You are here to experiment with Life itself so you may grow and evolve. The whole pointof this beautiful sacred gift of Beingness is to do just that.

Experiment to your heart's content, fail often and in all sorts of beautiful and poetic ways, then learn your lesson and suck the nectar of wisdom out of the experience, and do it all over again.

Man is most nearly himself when he achieves the seriousness of a child at play.

- Heraclitus -

So, here's a question for you: are you playing in/with Life, or are you grinding your way through it? If it's the latter, let me show you through this course how to make it play.

Our Magical Creative Cosmos Revealed.

So far, we've taken a pretty good plunge into discovering the science and mechanics of our Inner World. Fortunately, we won't need to cover as much ground to do the same for the Outer World.

The reason is that all your creative control lies within your Inner World. None of us have any sort of direct control over our Outer World, much like you don't have to do anything for a mirror to reflect back your image or likeness when you stand in front of it.

In broad strokes, the Outer World we experience as our reality can be understood as a holographic reflection of our Inner World.

The primary reason we don't have direct control is because we're not the only ones expressing into this Outer World. It's a co-created reality with all the other humans, animals, life forms, and everything else that makes up the infinite vastness of our Cosmos.

In other words, we're not the only likeness reflected into this mirror that produces the holographic reflection we experience as our reality. There's a coalescent interaction with all other forces and creative powers. And on top of all that, there are immutable laws that govern all of Creation.

It's safe to say this is all infinitely complex as there are billions upon billions of variables at play at all times, most of which we can't even see, know, account for, or let alone control or manipulate directly.

The Universe is a dream dreamed by a single dreamer where all the dream characters dream also.

- Arthur Schopenhauer -

The question then becomes what we can do to make sure our dream doesn't become a nightmare.

That's the question we're going to answer now, but I'll answer it first before going to the explanation why.

We don't need to be able to control or manipulate the Outer World directly to be able to co-create (i.e., manifest) the lived experiences we desire to bring into our Life.

We also don't need to know all the immutable laws that govern this entire Universe, which is a very good thing as I could write 80 volumes of profound books and still not do that topic justice or help you any further.

All we need to do is to learn to trust a few simple rules and learn a few immutable laws, then we're good to go as far manifestation is concerned. Here it goes:

Rule #1 - Everything is always in perfect order.

This Universe and all within it was created, is animated, and governed by an infinite intelligence in infinitely intelligent ways according to an infinitely intelligent design.

There are no such things as flukes, accidents, coincidences, or random events—ever. Underneath whatever chaos we might perceive in the manifest material world, there's always perfect order in the unmanifest fundamental reality that's lies at the foundation of everything in this Universe.

In the academic circles of quantum physics, this fundamental reality is referred to as the Unified Field, and in the 5,000-year-old Vedic tradition, it's called Brahman. Others call this Source Consciousness, but labels—as always—are unimportant.

LOVE+ TRUTH | dōjō

We're after understanding the concept not naming rights or preferences, so use whatever label resonates most with you.

So, whatever we might perceive as chaos in our reality is truthfully always in perfect order. The disconnect is that we don't understand how or why, but that doesn't negatethe fact that we can know—and therefore trust—that the entire Universe is indeed in perfect order at all times with zero exception.

Our personal reality might not be in perfect order from our vantage point, but we're merely a fractal of a totality we cannot comprehend as its vastness and complexity is beyond the computing limits of our Mind. We simply can't computeall the billions upon billions of variables at play at any given time—it's vastness and complexity will always be beyond our grasp.

Then there's judgment error as our lens is not perfectly clear with all our encultured conditioning. The aperture of our awareness might be open, but it's nowhere near so wide that we can comprehend all of Creation (except maybe the handful of us at the sage level but I promise you, if you're reading this you can rest assured that you're not yet at that level and for that matter neither am I). Here's the good news: if we can know and trust that

the Universe is always in perfectorder, we actually don't need to know all thesebillions upon variables or understand how it's in perfect order.

We can simply know and trust it is so. This means that whateveris showing up for us in our reality must be of this same quality—it simply cannot be any other way. The only question we need to examine is: "What was my part in the co-creation of this reality or lived experience, and what was due to factors unknown or beyond my control?"

Knowing and trusting this rule allows us to use it as a North Star that we can wisely navigate by.

We don't need to second-guess whether this outcome is fair, whether that result is normal, or whether something could have been different. We can simply embrace it as a reflection of perfect order. It is the inevitable outcome or result from all that co- created it in the first place.

With this knowing, we can then journey inwards and venture into our Inner World to discover if we may have made missteps or mistakes along the way. Maybe we waited too long or abandonedship too soon. Maybe we just weren't ready, or hadn't gained enough mastery in a skill or ability, whether

LOVE+ TRUTH | dōjō

43

it's a tangible skill or a mental/emotional one.

Maybe we were guided in our actions or inactions by fear, doubt, worry, or a sense of unworthiness. Whatever it might be, there are always answers and guidance to be discovered when we venture into our Inner World.

Rule #2 - Everything is always happening for our greatest growth, our greatest prosperity, and our greatest evolution.

This second rule builds on the first one but it layers in a very important nuance of understanding.

We live in a benevolent Universe even though our lived experiences at times can really challenge that knowing. When we experience gross violations or atrocities, our trust in this rule is severely challenged. In many cases, the logical conclusion might be to perceive this rule as false.

Yet, this rule always holds true even though—admittedly—it requires a courageous leap of spiritual faith to embrace it fully. The challenge is in our perception as we simply don't see the whole picture. We don't need to delve too deep into this rabbit hole, but suffice to say that the law of Karma crosses across all our lifetimes. Karmic debts incurred in previous lifetimes can and

sometimes must be paid in this lifetime while we incurred them in past ones.

Even in instances of the most grotesque violations or abuses, our Soul would have chosen this in our lifetime or it would not be possible to manifest.

Why and how a Soul might choose this is beyond this course. All I will share is that things work a little differently in the spiritual realm where earthly wealth, pleasure, comfort, or convenience are of minimal significance. The game Spirit plays is spiritual evolution, and some of these terrible lived experiences can translate into giant spiritual leaps in ripening and developing as a Soul.

The gem cannot be polished without friction, nor man without trials.

– Confucius –

The Truth is there's spiritual poetry in all lived experiences—the good, the bad, the ugly, and the sublime.

And, of course, when I speak of spiritual poetry I am really pointing at the effervescent beauty within the sole purpose of the existence of this Universe and all within in it: growth, prosperity, and evolution through infinite new experiences.

The only way to truly know this and not become an embittered cynic requires gaining a philosophical understanding of the deeper meaning of the words growth, prosperity, and evolution.

The core issue here is mankind's prevailing misunderstanding that things are either right or wrong, good or bad.

If we wish to ascend to higher levels of spiritual ripeness and maturity, we must gain mastery in holding the paradoxical nature of reality, as everything is in fact everything at all times.

Yes, that's a big threshold to cross. How can everything be possibly good and bad or right and wrong at the very same time?

Let me demonstrate this principle with an extreme example. Let's take Adolf Hitler, who we all can agree was a horrible tyrant that engineered unthinkable atrocities in the name of a hateful and patently false ideology.

Yet, after World War II, Western Europe united in a way that makes war among France or Germany or the United Kingdom completely unthinkable. This was no small leap

forward—since the dawn of civilization in that landmass we call Europe, there had been nothing but unceasing wars and violent conflicts. For thousands of years there was always some war or bloodshed going on.

That's an example of the paradoxical nature of reality: Hitler was unquestionably a horrible figure in history, and at the very same time, he was the catalyst for something that was profoundly positive for humanity.

Spiritual maturity is being able to hold the paradoxical nature of reality - to hold all vantage points on all occurrences.

Here's where I am going with all of this. We cannot see the words growth, prosperity, and evolution in the narrow definition of positive, good, or pleasant.

Some of the greatest spiritual leaps we'll make will come straight from the worst crises, catastrophes, or calamities we'll experience in life.

Knowing and embracing this is the pathway to discovering the spiritual poetry within even the "worst" things that happen to us.

Rule #2 can only be embraced, understood, and internalized in this rich philosophical understanding of the paradoxical nature of reality.

Without this expanded view of Life itself, we will not be able to see our way past "that" which on the surface cannot be seen in any other way but bad, wrong, terrible, horrible, tragic, grotesque, or atrocious.

Where all of this leads us with Rule #2 is the exact same place as Rule #1. We can know and trust this rule to be true at all times, so we can navigate by it and allow it to show us where we can discover the deeper lessons within our lived experiences.

Nothing happens to any man that he is not formed by Nature to bear.

- Marcus Aurelius -

As with all things, more practice cultivates more mastery, and so I encourage you to start putting both these rules to practice often and with vigor.

You will discover that deep within you is a vast reservoir of wisdom that will guide you through all the inherent trials and tribulations we each face during our lifetime because all things become bearable when their deeper purpose can be discovered and understood.

You are far more capable than you give yourself credit for, far stronger and resilient than you think, and far wiser than you know.

We don't need a gigantic Swiss army knife of rules to slice our way through life with wisdom and grace, all we need is these two rules and we're good to go so let's now explore the two Cosmic laws that are key to know.

Law #1 - The law of Least Effort.

I hope it is starting to become clear that Life itself is simple, just not easy. The rules and laws of all of Creation are plain and simple; they are never complicated and definitely not subject to some special codes or privileges that are accessible to some but not others.

Nope, they're available and accessible to each of us with zero exceptions—but only so long as we do the necessary work to cultivate the spiritual ripeness and maturity to access them.

We cannot put to work "that" which wedon't know or understand. Again, this is simple, just not always easy.

So it goes with the Law of Least Effort, which is very simple but many of us make it unnecessary difficult or complicated for ourselves. Often, we then falsely

LOVE+ TRUTH | dōjō

translate this unnecessary difficulty into the understanding that Life itself is "always" hard, nothing "ever" works out for me, and so on.

The Law of Least Effort states that at all times there'sa path available to us that requires the least amount of effort versus the countless paths where we have to expend a big effort.

Least effort in this contextis not to be confused with easy, convenient, or even pleasant, as the path of least effort can still be hard, inconvenient, or unpleasant at times.

The difference is how much energy it extracts from us. The path of least effort might be hard, inconvenient, or unpleasant, but it will not deplete our energy to the extent we're completely exhausted, worn out, or overwhelmed.

Conversely, when we're on any of the paths of big effort, the very same hardships, inconveniences, or unpleasantries will completely exhaust us, wear us out, and overwhelm us.

This is because Life is meant to be walked down the path of Least Effort, not Big Effort.

Hence, we have once again a marker to navigate by. When we

find ourselves drained of energy and worn out, and everything takes copious amounts of energy, then life is showing us we're not on our path of Least Effort. We're not being punished, and it's never that we're not good or worthy enough or that you were born with a pint of incurable Irish bad luck in your veins.

None of that, Life is merely showing us something - there's a lesson in all of this.

When you are on your path, and it's truly your path, doors will open for you where there were no doors for someone else.

- Joseph Campbell -

The law of least effort goes hand-in-hand with the next law I am going to introduce, but before I do, I'd like to share a big insight into why you might have at times chosen to walk the path of big effort.

Our society—the Matrix we live in, if you will—is designed and functions as a controlled environment.

Those in control of Power have a vision and ambition for society which is self-serving and perpetuates the "master-servant" model, which has been the bedrock of human civilization since antiquity.

This is not a diehard "truther" statement, conspiracy theory, or the words of a political activist, as I am none of those. I am stating facts which we can readily observe when we are willing to gain eyes for it. All of this is anchored in anthropology, political science, and the Neoclassical theory of free markets economics.

There are three predominant objectives thosein power have to ensure the servant class remains indentured and beholden to the larger system they function within.

To sway this away from terms like the "elites" and make this more impersonal, I am going to refer to those in power as the "System"from here on out.

Note that "servants" here refers to the vast majority of people as less than 1% is truly in power and all others are—mostly unbeknownst to themselves—servants to the System.

Incidentally, this includes very wealthy people, doctors, lawyers, politicians, titans of industry, and so on, so don't confuse "servants" to mean only those on the bottom ranks of society. It extends all the way to very close to the very top.

The first objective is continuous disempowerment.

The System does not want you to know your actual creative powers as if you would know, you would want to break free from the System and no longer obey its objectives.

The System does this systematically through forms of relentless messaging, propaganda, and the creation of narratives and storylines that are designed to impart the overarching belief that you, as an individual, are powerless and cannot change the way the world simply is.

The narrative is always to show you the world is a very dangerous place, and you need the structures of big business, government institutions, laws, intelligence agencies, armies that can wage wars, to be safe and protected for the great dangers that live "out there."

Our entire modern-day education system is designed to groom loyal servants that can pass a

48

meaningless test but have no command of sovereign critical thought. The System doesn't want you to truly think; they want you to become a useful cog-in-the-wheel in service to the System.

A vital part of this disempowerment objective is executed via the age-old Roman maxim "give them bread and circuses and they will never revolt."

There's a reason the System ensures you are stimulated and distracted with celebrities, an endless stream of drama and violent movies and binge-watching meaningless TV shows, social media, sport voyeurism, gambling, and why alcohol consumption is legal and advertised as normal while it's as bad or worse for your health as cigarettes.

There's a reason Western medicine is centered around pharmaceutical intervention as it renders you into a position of life-long pharma-doctor dependency.

I can keep going, but every facet of the System is designed to make sure you remain an indentured servant, no matter how much you might believe you escaped the System by rising in wealth and social class.

You cannot escape the System on the material plane, the only way out is through the spiritual realm where you rise above its vice grip and now it just becomes a playground for you to frolic around with form and creation.

So, in an ironic twist of language, the way out of being a servant to

the System is not becoming one of its masters, but instead gaining mastery of ourselves.

Once we reawaken to our true creative powers endowed to us by virtue of our Divine origins, we are on our way to being free.

The second objective is to seed continuous envy and lack.

The System needs you pacified from wanting to challenge, or worse, rebel against it. At the same time, for the System to function and perpetuate itself, it needs you to be always hungry and craving for more.

It needs you to endlessly consume so you will work for the System. It wants you to incur debts to consume beyond your actual means so you become even more beholden to it. It creates this desire within you to make you want things you don't really need.

All luxury brands, cars, high fashion, cosmetics, plastic surgery, exclusive private clubs, or even communities are all designed around the false premise and empty promise that these are the epitome of a successful and happy life.

Celebrities, professional athletes, influencers, or whatever other form of "star" or "superstar" are paraded around like live mannequins and advertised as the lifestyle to emulate and desire. A whole apparatus of gossip media, social media, TV shows, award shows, and of course advertising is then used to continuously seed envy and lack.

The core message of all it is that "the grass is greener elsewhere" so you never stop chasing the next fix of dopamine.

Liberation from this circus can only come in one way: release all your desires and cravings for "that" which you truly don't need. Of course, this is once again a leap in spiritual ripening and maturity as we need to surrender our childish "wants" for that we truly need to live a fulfilled life.

This doesn't mean we can't have any of these goodies—we can have as many big houses, fancy cars, or shiny objects as we wish, as there are no Cosmic laws against living an abundant life. What needs to go is our false belief these "things" will complete or fulfill us in meaningful ways.

You'll likely find that in surrendering the craving for the things you don't really need or aren't healthy for you, the seductive lure will in time dissipate entirely. We start seeing the folly in all of it, and when we arrive at that place within our

Inner World, we can truly play with all these things in our Outer World versus being consumed and owned by it.

The third objective is to pull you back and forth between the past and future continuously.

The System knows that all of Creation takes place exclusively in the present moment, and that all your innate creative powers will inevitably come alive if you could only stay in the present moment long and often enough.

Incidentally, in case you were wondering, I am going to bring all of this back to the Law of Least Effort.

Hence, the System wants you distracted and pulled out of the present moment and does so by yo-yoing you back and forth between the past and future.

For the past, it will tell you alluring stories of the grand ol' days full of epic fairytales of heroism, brave feats, and great accomplishments. It wants you to long for the past, and it will do so by romanticizing it

LOVE+ TRUTH | dōjō

to the extent it resembles nothing like what really ever happened or existed.

At the same time, it wants you to fear the future. This secures the need for the System to continue to exist, as only the System can protect you from the grave dangers it conjures up to be ahead. All fearmongering around imminent geopolitical threats or possible wars which then justifies the build-up of a massive intelligence agency and defense apparatus is all anchored in seeding fear for the future.

It's gone so far as the world's so-called superpowers building up a nuclear arms arsenal which is capable of destroying the planet one hundred times over. It is complete and utter madness, but collectively we all buy into it as the future is full of danger, so they tell us.

Or could it be these very people telling us this story make it so?

All is known in the sacredness of silence.

- Rumi -

The way out of allowing yourself to be yo-yoed back and forth from the past to the future is to consciously and decisively step into and anchor yourself in the present moment.

This requires cultivating the quality of presence as well as embracing the silence deep within our Inner World as a refuge from the incessant noise imposed on us by the Outer World.

Now let's take all of this back to the Law of Least Effort.

The direct connection is that the System will at all times attempt to sway you to go on its path, which is not necessarily your unique path.

Only your unique path—that path which will lead you to the realization of your unique dreams and aspirations, not what the world tells you should do or be—will offer you the extraordinary benefit of the Law of Least Effort.

If you are on your unique path, you might work countless hours but it will never feel like work. You might face many challenges and stumble many times, but it will never feel to you as mountains that can't be scaled or oceans that can't be crossed.

This is the Law of Least Effort—all you need to do is find your Dharma and go in that direction.

It's that simple, just not always easy as the world has a way of fooling you into doing what the System wants you to do and be.

Law #2 - The Law of Dharma

The Law of Dharma is also profound it its simplicity and elegance. Dharma is a rich Sanskrit word which like many other Sanskrit words has a multitude of meanings in Vedic texts and ancient wisdom traditions. In the context of this law, we're referring to Dharma with the meaning "purpose in life."

Just like none of us are identical, we each have a unique Dharma that only we can bring to life and express onto the canvas of all of Creation in the way we're meant to.

All of creation and Life itself thrives on diversity. We see it everywhere in Nature where not a single tree, plant, insect, or animal is exactly the same. They might be of the same species, but you will not find a single exact duplicate of anything in Nature. This is by intelligent design as diversity creates perfect harmony and progression whereas uniformity breeds stagnation and then decline as far as evolution is concerned.

So, let's state the obvious: you are designed, created, and meant to be you and nobody else.

The Outer World might like you to be in conformity, if not uniformity, with its ideals and aspirations for you, but Nature simply doesn't operate that way. Nature (read: the Most High) has its own plans for every single "thing" within all of Creation. Yes, you and I are merely a speck of divine stardust within all of Creation. No amount of protest or debate will ever change this.

Our maybe 80-90 years here on Earth is a fractionof a nanosecond within the entire evolutionary process of this Universe.

Embracing this with humility and reverence for where each of us fits in is very liberating and will unburden you from any grandiose ideas we might have about our own importance.

At the same time—here wesee the paradoxical nature of reality once again—you are vitally important to all of Creation and your Dharma is a big part of that.

If you were not supposed to be here, you simply wouldn't. So, you must be needed, it cannot be any other way.

Without you here, all of Creation would not be complete or in harmony, which means it would be in a state of chaos and that's not possible as everything is always in perfect order.

LOVE+ TRUTH | dōjō

Clearly then, you are here for a purpose. There's meaning to you being here on the earthly plane at this exact time in history, born into this family, in this country, and so on.

It's all by Divine design and orchestration whether or not we can see it, understand it, or even ever come to know it.

So whether you can embracethat truth at this time or not, let's run with it because the law of Dharma is premised on this understanding.

The notion of Dharma is some of the finest spiritual poetry you'll ever encounter but it does require a leap of faith to embrace the belief that there is a Creator—whatever we might call or label it—that is a unified omniscient creative power at the origin and woven into all Creation.

In Hermetic philosophy, this notion is captured in the following axiom:

"While All is in The All, it is equally true that The All is in All."

This axiom is accentuated with the guidance: "To him who truly understands this Truth hath come great knowledge."

Of course, "The All" is just another linguistic label for what is also called God, Creator, Source, Great Spirit, Yahweh, Brahman, Oversoul, and countless other names all pointing at the very same "thing."

"All" refers to everything in all of creation or whatever is contained within the Universe including the Universe itself. We are just one

little humble expression of life itself in a Universe which overflows with creations of all kinds.

What this really means is that "The All" is alive and living through "All," and so there's your nucleus of Divinity if you ever wondered about it.

Moreover, your life is not merely yours. Something far grander is experiencing its own creation through the creation of you. It's experiencing it from the unique vantage point which is you, and The All cannot gain that exact and unique vantage point of all its creation except through you.

You are irreplaceable and of essential importance in all of its Creation, and so are the desires, dreams, and aspirations you wish to bring into your lived experience. The only way for The All to experience the realization of these is through you realizing them.

Maybe read that again, as I promise you I am not blowing a bunch of spiritual hot air up your you-know-what. This Truth—should you decide to see it—will cure you of so much confusion and mental delusion that I can't even start to list its medicinal benefits.

Here's why: as I explained earlier, this entire Universe and all of Creation is created, animated, and orchestrated by an infinite intelligence according to an infinitely intelligent design and it's doing so at all times in infinitely intelligent ways. This is why everything is always in perfect order, even when it might appear to us as chaotic at times.

Such an omniscient and omnipotent creative power would not make a design mistake in you or me.

Hence, we can know with absolute certainty and conviction that we have all the gifts, talents, superpowers, and access to the resources we need to realize our Dharma.

All we truly need to do is go on the journey of realization knowing that we already possess everything we need, and the specific chance encounters, circumstances and serendipities required for us to reach our Destiny will manifest themselves at the perfect time.

The only place where all this runs off the tracks is if we don't know our Dharma, or if we do know, if we

do not follow it.

In Joseph Campbell's words: "We must follow our bliss."

So, let's see why either of those scenarios might come into our reality. The first one—we don't know our Dharma—is fairly simple to solve while the second one - we don't follow it - requires a bit more explanation.

The first one is the true dream you hold for you in your heart. It's impossible not to discover it, as we all have dreams and aspirations. But it is easy to get confused when we allow our Mind to interfere.

Our Mind will always seed doubt, worry, and fear about whatever it doesn't know. Your dreams and aspirations are by definition unknown, as they wouldn't be true dreams and aspirations if they were already a lived experience.

The solution is very simple. You must go on the journey of realizing and actualizing your dreams and aspirations. This course will help you with that, but what this course cannot do is discover and embrace your dreams and aspirations for you. You will have to do that, as nobody but you can know what's truly in your Heart.

The greatest trap door is knowing the difference between intrinsically motivated desires, dreams, and aspirations and extrinsically motivated ones.

Intrinsically motivated ones are what's truly in your heart. That's your Dharma whispering to you.

Extrinsically motivated ones are what the world told you that you should desire. They will always be something the System imposes upon you so you stay an obedient and indentured servant.

The System will tell you that your salvation is in accumulating fame, fortune, applause, trophies, and shiny objects. There's nothing inherently wrong with any of those, but by themselves, they will never fulfill you in meaningful ways for any significant duration of time.

There's simply no bliss to be found in them. At best, you will be stuck (or lost) at the level of pleasure, convenience, and fleeting moments of superficial happiness.

Your Dharma are those whispers that are tugging at your soul to be realized. They might not make any

sense to anyone but you—and more likely than not, even you might have your doubts as to whether it's realistic for you to realize or actualize "that" which the whispers keep telling you.

Trust it. Your Mind might play tricks and games, but your Heart knows and will never steer you the wrong way.

Do not compare, do not measure. No other way is like yours. All other ways deceive and tempt you. You must fulfill the way that is in you.

- Carl Gustav Jung -

Your task is to cultivate the discernment whether what you dream or aspire to is intrinsically motivated or something that the world informed you would be best, logical, or achievable for you.

That takes care of the first problem of not knowing our Dharma, so what about knowing it but not trusting it and choosing another path?

Here is where we can use the Law of Least Effort to discern whether we're in alignment with the Law of Dharma.

If it depletes your energy, feels like hard work, or bores you to tears, you can know it's not your Dharma.

If you feel unfulfilled, or empty, or restless, or depressed, or worse, suicidal, you can know you are not following your true calling and purpose in life. If what you're pursuing is motivated extrinsically or to please others, you're not following your Dharma.

If you are lost in stimulation and addictions such as alcohol, drugs, painkillers, anti-depressants, binge eating, binge watching, gambling, consumerism, gluttony, debauchery, porn, sex, or whatever other form of escapism and numbing, then you are simply not on your Dharmic path.

This is all fairly simple, just not easy as we succumbed to all these things because we have a void inside of us. More often than not, this is not because we're weak or incapable; it's because the world just never taught us any of these things. All we know is that we're not happyor fulfilled and we discovered that these "escapes" helped us numb the pain inside.

What they also do is quell our ability to hear the whispers of our Heart, as these are soft and subtle whereas our Mind is loud and very vocal.

All forms of escapism and numbing drown out the soft whispers of our Heart, so if this is the case for you, the solution is to wean off the addictions and everything else that you use to numb your inner suffering. It's not easy, but you either choose yourself and go on this arduous cleansing journey, or you will simply sink deeper and deeper into inner suffering until it becomes so unbearable you have no choice left.

I say all of this with the greatest compassion. I know all of this because I have been there. I've been to that dark place; I know how difficult and hard it can be to escape the quicksand of our own suffering when there seemsno way out.

I promise you there is, and this course—if taken seriously and done in earnest—can be a lifeline. I will help you and lend you my strength and regained buoyancy so you can lift yourself up, but you must grab my hand and allow me to guide you. Through my countless missteps and mistakes, I did finally discover at least one path out of darkness. There are undoubtedly others, but this is the one I know.

With all of that said, we have just two rules and two laws we need in our spiritual toolkit to start navigating this magical, creative

LOVE+ TRUTH | dōjō

Cosmos with skill, agility, precision, intelligence, and grace.

It's all simple, just not always easy.

Next up we will explore the concept of Intelligence, the last keystone we need to be ready to take on this course.

About Intelligence.

To truly take this course to the level of depth I aspire to, I would be remiss to not include a deeper exploration of intelligence.

This is because all of us know the word "intelligence," but humanity's prevailing understanding of intelligence is heavily skewed and incomplete.

The prevailing understanding is that intelligence is a measure of acuity or "smarts." We often associate this with a standardized IQ test, which measures a very limited set of capabilities of our logical Mind.

Nothing could be further from the truth. An IQ test merely measures our level of accessible brainpower, which is a vastly different quality than our intelligence.

Brainpower itself is very much like an engine which has raw horse-power potential and readily accessible horsepower. The raw potential is the output it's capable

of, the readily accessible horsepower is what it can actually produce or access in the moment.

Finally, some of us are born with more raw horsepower potential than others, but that doesn't mean anything if it goes unrealized.

All of that is just brainpower, which for this course and Life itself is not nearly as consequential as being able to readily access our innate intelligence.

So, what then is intelligence?

From the perspective of the Universe—which is the only perspective that truly matters—intelligence is defined as "that" which produces intelligent outcomes, while intelligent outcomes are themselves defined as those outcomes which are conducive to Life itself.

Unintelligent outcomes—those not conducive to Life itself—originate then by definition from unintelligence.

In other words, intelligence always leads to outcomes which are Life-affirming and outcomes which are anti-Life by definition stem from unintelligence.

All forms of war, violence, hate, racism, bigotry, socially engineered inequalities or injustices, famine,

57

pollution, exploitation, degradation, degeneration, and addictions just to name a few are all examples of unintelligent out- comes as they are all unmistakenly anti-Life in nature.

Here we can clearly see that brainpower is a vastlydifferent entity or quality than intelligence.

This is because you can have all the readily accessible brainpower in the world—as most who control and govern our world do—and still create an overwhelming number of deeply unintelligent outcomes.

Hence, brainpower and intelligence are two very different qualities. We can have oodles of brainpower and little access to intelligence, and perhaps moderate brainpower but exemplary access to intelligence.

Brainpower means very little unless it's rooted in intelligence. In fact, it's a grave danger when not rooted in intelligence. This is the great problem facing humanity with A.I., given that people with great brainpower and little intelligence are the current engineers of A.I.

Of course, we can also have great brainpower and full access to our innate intelligence, and these are the people we could rightfully classify as the very rare true geniuses among us. Typically we don't recognize them as such and label them as a sage or mystic

instead. You can typically spot them quite easily—if you can find them—by their complete disinterest in popularity and power or control over others. This makes them ideally suited to be the leaders in places of power and influence; yet, somewhat ironically, their complete detachment from the lust for power usually translates into them fulfilling their Dharma in comparatively anonymous ways.

Conversely, the world or System labels anyone with merely great brainpower as a genius and promotes them into the various places of power and influence across government, business, finance, medicine, science, and academia.

This is the crux of why the world today looks the way it does - what we're missing is intelligence.

With that in mind, let'sexplore a deeper understanding of intelligence.

We'll focus only on those aspects most relevant for this course, as intelligence is a subject with vast depths. But again, we're not after a PhD, just a practical field guide which can give us quick and tangible results.

The first aspect of intelligence to grasp is that it's not just a singular entity; instead, it's a harmonious

LOVE+
TRUTH | dōjō

convergence of various intelligences that "reside" at different levels of density within the totality of our human avatar.

The simplest way to visualize or understand this is that we have a level of intelligence that resides, functions, and operates at the level of Body, Emotions, Mind, and Heart.

There are several more intelligences we have access to, but I'll touch on that when we get into the intelligence of the Heart.

For ease of absorbing this information, let's stick to the four levels which are recognizable to each of us.

I am not going to dwell too much on the intelligence of the physical Body, as this intelligence functions almost entirely autonomously and outside of our conscious direction.

Our bodies each have an estimated 30-40 trillion cells which all communicate, exchange information, and self-regulate the entire complex living system that is our human body. It knows how to digest food, regulate hormones, heal wounds, detect and fight viruses and harmful pathogens, and so on.

Every fraction of a second, the intelligence of our Body executes and orchestrates billions of micro-

decisions across all 30-40 trillion cells. It's nothing short of miraculous.

There's also not a supercomputer in the world that could possibly do—in real-time—what the intelligence of our Body does without any conscious involvement on our part.

This intelligence is awe-inspiring, but since it functions entirely autonomously, we don't need to know much else about it except that this intelligence—like all other ones we're going to cover—is interdependent with all other levels of intelligence within the human avatar.

A seeker of Truth looks beyond the apparent and contemplates the hidden.

- Rumi-

The next level in density from our Body are our Emotions. This is actually a step-down in density as with Emotions we already enter the unmanifest ethereal realm whereas the Body "resides" in the manifest material realm.

However, the intelligence of our Emotions still viscerally expresses itself as our Body directly interacts and responds to our Emotions. Just think of our facial expressions, which are a direct and undeniable expression of how we feel in the moment regardless how well you believe you can "poker face" your way through Life.

The reality is your eyes,mouth, skin tone, eyebrows, or frowns can't truly lie. A happy face looks very different from a sad or angry face, and all of this is your emotions expressing themselves.

As discussed, the intelligence of the Body is dispersed across every cell and has no obvious central command center. The intelligence of our Emotions works in a similar way with the notable exception that our emotional intelligence command center is in our gut.

So, when we speak of "feeling it in our gut" or gut intelligence, we're really pointing at our Emotional intelligence. I should note that our gut intelligence does vastly more, but that's not a concern for us in this course.

The intelligence of our Emotions operates multi-dimensionally. It's not only in direct symbiotic relation with our Body and Mind, but it's also a voracious collector of data and inputs from the Outer World,

which it does throughsensing and feeling into the sphere directly outside of our Body.

As it operates at the distinct frequency field of all emotions, the data it collects is of that same frequency range and then, in symbiotic relationship, this "raw" data of an emotional quality is passed along to our Mind which translates that data in thoughts, opinions, etc.

All of this happens seamless and instantaneously when we have cultivated mastery in accessing the intelligence of our Emotions.

Regretfully, with the onset of the scientific revolution in the 1600s, the intelligence of our Emotions was devalued as inconsequential as humanity was having a love affair with the logical Mind.

In modern Western civilization, Emotional intelligence has no place in the curriculum in the school system. Most parents themselves are inept at best so they can't teach it either, and society as a whole simply doesn't value it.

The astoundingly high rate of alcoholism, drug use, anti-depressants, and other addictions would all be substantially lower if Emotional intelligence were widely taught in schools and recognized as highly valuable by society. The root

LOVE+ TRUTH | dōjō

cause of all these ailments is that people feel disconnected from their true Self (i.e. their Soul essence, not their small self or Ego), the people closest to them, and the entire world around them. The internet and social media has only worsened this sense of disconnect, and any sort of escapism into virtual reality will only aggravate this misery because we're social animals.

We crave connection, and we are "designed" to live in pods. The convergence of all this desocialization, alienation, and isolation is much like an orca or dolphin kept in captivity who slowly wither away until they die a sad, lonely, and often premature death.

So, cultivating and embracing the immeasurable value and importance of the intelligence of our Emotions is a station we must pass through if we wish to ripen in spiritual maturity, but it's not central to this course.

At the next step-down in density we encounter the intelligence of our Mind.

We already explored the Mind earlier, so we don't need to spend too much time on this third quality of intelligence we possess within us.

What is helpful to know is that our Mind is made up of three distinct

"brains" which each have their own unique function and capabilities.

The oldest and smallest part of our brain is the reptilian brain, which houses our survival and animal instincts. It lays mostly dormant until it gets triggered into "on mode" through a signal from the amygdala that there's a clear and present danger.

People in acute fear, anger, or rage all were triggered somehow, and then their reptilian brain took over the controls. Their actions and reactions in this brain mode are instinctive; what they do or say then while in this mode is outside their "normal" behavior. Literally, they went "unconscious" until they snap out of it.

There's no point in engaging with these people as they're not receptive to logic or reason, as they are simply not aware or conscious to the brain mode they are in. Best just to leave or escape the situation.

The next level is the limbic brain. The limbic brain's primary function is to process how we feel about something, but it does so in a very different way than the intelligence of our Emotions.

Interestingly enough, scientific research has now shown that we make most of our decisions with our limbic brain rather than our prefrontal cortex (i.e. our logical "brain") as was always thought. We analyze and synthesize information with our logical brain but then, when all is said and done, the final decision so to speak is passed on to our Limbic Brains which makes a decision about it based on how it feels about the logical analysis and conclusions that were processed by our pre-frontal cortex.

Advertisers know this very well, virtually all astute marketing and advertising is designed to sway and influence your Limbic Brain, far less your logical brain.

For instance, if McDonalds tried to sell you on their quality, benefits, or value of their food through the logical brain you wouldn't buy it - Jamie Oliver won a lawsuit against them with his claim their food is unfit for human consumption.

Yet, McDonald's is one of the largest food chains in the world as their marketing has nothing to do with their food. They sell you on the illusion there's a lot of "happiness" in their meals.

It is the same with Coca-Cola. Gucci sells you on the illusion (or delusion, come to think of it) that having one of their over-priced bags hanging off your shoulders will give you social status and make you more successful. This means nothing to

your logical brain as it cannot compute that concept, but your limbic brain can readily process that messaging and—if it perceives that as a valuable or desirable feeling - it will buy the delusion hook, line, and sinker.

The third and final level brain is our logical brain, which as we just mentioned resides in our prefrontal cortex. This is our analytical mind which processes and computes copious amounts of data flooding in and then assigns meaning or draws conclusions. It regulates many more functions, but that's the part we care most about.

All three of these levels make up our entire brain, and what we call our Mind is an amalgamation of these three levels with their distinct functions and capabilities.

For the avoidance of doubt, when I referred to the Mind as I did in prior sections of this book, I was referring to the whole assembly of these three levels of brain.

The preceding discussion of the three levels of brain was not to provide you with trivial information but to set-up a foundational understanding that can help us bridge how the intelligence of the Mind fundamentally differs from the intelligence of the Heart. The crux of that difference is that the intelligence of the Mind is "capped"

LOVE+ TRUTH | dōjō

by logic or rational thinking which is linear in nature.

The intelligence of the Heart is suprarational in nature which means inclusive of rational thought yet beyond—in other words, the intelligence of the Heart gives us access to non-linear intelligence. And, since we now know from advances in quantum physics that our Universe cannot be fully understood unless we also accept and embrace its non-linearity, we have the perfect segue to dive into the last and perhaps most important part of this self-study material.

All of this brings us to where I really wanted to take you: the intelligence of the Heart.

The intelligence of our Heartis not just where we can access the greatest depth of intelligence available to us as humans; it's the portal to access the deep wisdom of our Soul.

Let's start with intelligence in general, as many believe our Mind is the sole source of all our computing powers. The Mind is indeed a marvel of Divine ingenuity and capable of truly mesmerizing feats. Nevertheless, as just mentioned our Mind is limited to the domain of logic and reason. Many will argue with this, claiming the

right hemisphere of our brain is our "creative and non-linear" sphere and capable of amazing wizardry well beyond the confines of logic and reason.

This assertion is based on brain research where they measure which areas of the brain "lights up" when we're in a certain brainwave state as we are performing certain brain functions.

So far, so good. Except, it's an incomplete understanding. Let me explain why because it's helpful to know for where we're going with all of this. Afterward, you can choose to believe whatever suits you best.

The link conventional science is missing—as it doesn't understand and therefore can't recognize it—is where these creative ideas, dreams, imaginations, or other non-linear geniuses originate from.

All that's claimed to be "produced" by the right hemisphere of the brain actually originates from the quantum field, or what I refer to as the Infinite Field of Consciousness.

So how do I know?

In 2015, I experienced a profound spontaneous spiritual awakening and my claircognizance came online full throttle. At the time, I didn't have the faintest idea why I was suddenly "knowing" things without being able to logically explain why.

I was a diehard Ivy league educated businessman at the time, and the world of logic and reason was my bedrock. So I went on a journey of discovery and after years going deep into this subject, I synthesized a deeper understanding of the innate gifts we are all hardwired with.

I studied the latest we know in neuroscience, studied the gifts of sages and mystics, and eventually became a Certified Medium.

In this search, I stumbled upon the work of the HeartMath Institute, a highly reputable institute that has been doing robust scientific research focused entirely on Heart intelligence. At that time, this was the missing link that completed the picture for me logically, meaning my Mind could now grasp it. Later still, I would discover the understanding I share here is hardly unique to me as this "knowing" is as old as antiquity.

I share all the above only to provide the context for the information I am about the share and the source of my knowing. Since I've gone on the journey of mastering my gifts of claircognizance and channeling, I no longer constrain myself to the edges of conventional science

because all the yet unknown—or magic, if you will— is science we don't know or understand yet.

In all the ancient wisdom teachings of those we refer to as sages, mystics, seers, or holy avatars of which there have been a great many, all of them—in the words and language of their time—said, spoke, and pointed at the same "knowing" I am sharing here.

So, let's connect the dots and then you can choose to run with it or not.

First, the function that conventional science has traditionally assigned to the right hemisphere of the brain has since been called into question to such an extent that there are now opposing camps within the scientific community.

Turns out, advances in our understanding of how the brain works show the two hemispheres function more as redundant duplicates than was previously thought. We know this from people who had traumatic brain damage in one hemisphere and the "lost" functions then replicated themselves in the still intact hemisphere.

We also know that in a certain percentage of the population the brain hemispheres are reversed, even though science can't explain

LOVE+ TRUTH | dōjō

why. These are just two examples, but there are countless more.

For this course we don't care to know, I only shared these two to hopefully open you up to what I am about to share.

From the incredible research work done by the HeartMath Institute, we know there's not only a vast network of neurons around our Heart that produce measurable brainwave activity. We also know there's vastly more data going from the Heart to the Mind than the other way around.

We also know that the intelligence of our Heart has its own language, which is feeling, sensing, intuiting, and direct knowing.

In other words, it reads, receives, processes, and synthesizes information—which is data—in a different "language" than our Mind whose language is grammatical language and imagery.

So, here's the crux of it. Our Mind (regardless of brain hemisphere) functions as an "inverter" for the data it receives from the Heart.

One way to understand this is how solar panels work. Solar panels produce "direct current" energy, which we refer to as DC, yet our electrical grid and all households are wired to run on "alternating current," or AC. This makes solar energy not directly usable and this is why every solar panel installation includes an inverter which transforms the DC into AC, which then makes the solar energy usable and readily available.

When science measures brainwave activity and sees the right hemisphere light up, what it's really registering is data from the Heart being "inverted" to words and imagery which is "usable" and "readily available" to us.

I admit this by itself is a somewhat unsatisfactory explanation. It was for me, at least, so we must go a layer deeper as this begs the next question: why does this data which we believed to be the product of our creative right hemisphere come from the Heart?

The simple answer is because our Mind—or Heart, for that matter—can't by itself "produce" any of the original and creative ideas, dreams, aspirations, or imaginations we like to believe it can.

This is because everything already exists as a potentiality in the Unified Field. Humans have never invented or created anything original. All we're capable of doing is discovering something that always —literally for eternity—has existed in the Infinite Field of Consciousness, or what they call

Brahman in Vedic traditions and Great Spirit in indigenous wisdom

traditions. It's all the same thing we're pointing at, Unified Field is just the preferred term adopted by quantum physicists in their jargon.

You're not a mere drop in the ocean, you are the entire ocean in a drop.

- Rumi-

With everything already being a potentiality in the Unified Field, every single one of the infinite amount of potentialities has a distinct energy signature - or frequency and vibration - and as we covered earlier, when we come into sympathetic resonance with it, this potentiality occurs to us as a possibility.

In other words, that brilliant creative "idea" you or anyone else has, really is a potentiality in the Unified Field you connected with.

Mozart's music, Leonardo da Vinci's art and inventions, Einstein's scientific discoveries, Steve Jobs' idea for the iPod—it really doesn't matter, all of it existed as a potentiality in the Unified Field until

they "connected" with it as a possibility and then went about the process of manifesting it into the Earthly realm. Incidentally, this has not just been the knowing of sages and mystics since antiquity, and it's not some hocus pocus spiritual hypothesis, although some might argue it is.

One of the most brilliant quantum physicists of the 20th century was David Bohm, who Einstein called his spiritual son. Bohm produced a body of work called Bohmian Mechanics (also called the Brogli-Bohm Theory), which centered around the premise of non-local nature of the fundamental reality that underpins the material world we can observe.

That's a lot of fancy words, but what it means in plain English is that consciousness is non-local. It's not bound by time or space, it can and is at all places at all times.

If that didn't stretch your Mind yet, the next part might. You and I are a unique fractal of Source Consciousness expressed into a human avatar. Even though we're a unique fractal (think "aspect"), each fractal is still fundamentally of the same essence of this Source Consciousness. So by definition, it must have these same fundamental qualities—it cannot be any other way.

What, are you now telling me I am non-local?

Yes, you and I are non-local and at the same time we're here on the earthly plane experiencing life in and through our human avatar.

This rabbit hole goes even deeper, but I'll spare you this as for this course we're really only concerned with manifesting mastery through our human avatar here on the earthly plane.

However, we do need to connect all of this with the intelligence of the Heart as that's the understanding we're after.

Our Heart can be seen as an inter-dimensional portal that enables us to connect and interface with the Unified Field.

In Vedic traditions, what's referred to as our "Atman" or loosely translated "our seat of the Soul," is what's called our High or Spiritual Heart. When you see depictions of Jesus Christ with the Sacred Heart (the one with a cut and barbed wire around it) you'll notice this is placed in the middle, slightly above the sternum.

What we traditionally refer to as the location of the Heart chakra is slightly beneath this, but we actually have two Heart chakras (or, if you prefer, one Heart chakra with

two distinct aspects, same thing really) and the higher placed one is our seat of our Atman, Spiritual Heart, or Sacred Heart in Christianity.

Incidentally, our High or Spiritual Heart is associated with the Thymus gland in our biological Body—those of you familiar with the ancient practice of tapping the Thymus gland to arouse energy can now connect those dots as the seat of our Soul is also the wellspring of our Life Force energy. I am sharing all these factoids just to demonstrate this "knowledge" has been known since the dawn of time by various ancient wisdom traditions in all corners of the world at vastly different eras.

Hence, dismissing all of this as somehow coincidental or a fluke is certainly one choice, but I am inviting you to open up to it as this understanding will pay you great spiritual dividends in the long run.

Our High or Spiritual Heart serves as a portal into the unmanifest metaphysical dimensions where all infinite potentialities already exist. In fact, everything there is to know about everything that ever was, is currently, or can possibly exist is stored as information in the Unified Field.

When speak of our "Soul" we typically do so assuming this unique fractal of consciousness that "we" are reincarnated holistically (meaning lock, stock, and barrel) in our human avatar and is "stuck" within this physical entity called our Body until we die and then the Soul moves back to "the other side."

This is also an incomplete understanding as this simply can't be true if we accept the premise that all consciousness—fractal or otherwise—is non-local.

A more complete understanding is that an aspect of our unique fractal of Consciousness—our Soul, if you will—takes on the reincarnation of our human avatar, but another aspect of our Soul remains in the "form" of non-local consciousness in the metaphysical realm.

We call this aspect our Higher Self, and this is our source of our Higher Knowing as this aspect of our Soul is not bound or limited by the incarnation in this lifetime, in this human avatar, in this dense dimension of the material realm which we then experience as our reality.

Existing as non-local consciousness in the realm of non-locality, our Higher Self has access to all information and all potentialities across all timelines and all dimensions. If you'd like, you can think of the Higher Self as the wise sage within each of us.

It's this Higher Self aspect of our own Soul that acts as a conduit (to the Quantum Field) which then directly interacts and communicates with and through our High or Spiritual Heart. It's feeding it information so to speak.

Our Heart, as the portal and access point of this Higher Knowing, then passes this information on to our Mind, which translates ("inverts") this data into language and imagery we can work with at the level of Mind.

Every precognition, intuition, or direct knowing that "occurs" to us made this journey (so to speak) from the non-local Unified Field into our non-local Higher Self, which then communicated this information inter-dimensionally (from the non-local metaphysical realm into our human avatar which lives in the material realm) through our Heart.

The Heart passes this data onward to the Mind, which then translates the data into language and imagery we can understand and work with.

It gets even better, as it works in reverse also. We can "fetch" data such as information, ideas, guidance, or direction. All we need to do is cultivate mastery in the intelligence of the Heart, which starts by becoming fluent in its language which is feeling, sensing, intuiting, and direct knowing.

LOVE+ TRUTH | dōjō

A channeler or true "psychic," for instance, has cultivated this capability, but we all have the basic hardwiring factory-installed to be able to master this. Be aware, of course, of false prophets as many pretending to have mastery are just con artists.

You can know by the tapping into the intelligence of your Heart as you can sense into it. With some practice, you'll gain proficiency or even mastery, and you'll discover your Higher Self will give you crystal-clear answers and guidance with flawless accuracy.

Your Heart knows the way, run in that direction.

- Rumi-

The Sufi mystic, saint, and poet Rumi definitely knew all of this; his body of literary work is a treasure trove of wisdom of the Heart cloaked in effervescently beautiful poetry.

What Rumi knew, and you can find it within all his writings, is that when we get cut off from our Heart, we literally go soulless which is to say we become mechanical in nature.

When we get cut off from our Heart, we get cut off from our spark of Divinity. When this happens, the Mind—without the guidance and connection of our Higher Self—is capable of horrendous atrocities and is prone to adopt many misgivings about Life itself as it becomes mechanical – which is to say Heartless – in nature.

This is why the world today looks the way it does—humanity at-large has been cut off from the Heart, and the reality it has been creating is becoming progressively more sterile, mechanistic, and robotic—or, in other words, more and more soulless.

I could write volumes on the why and how, but for this course I am merely trying to bring you a basic understanding.

Admittedly, I've had many doubts and trepidations whether to share this inner sanctum of Higher Knowing.

The thought of supercharging anyone's manifesting powers and for that to only create more of what the world looks like today pains my Soul.

But I am going to trust you will read the next passage also and hopefully I can spark something inside of you, as I know it's within each of us.

We each must bring back our Soul's knowing on all levels. The only way to access this Higher Knowing within us is through the intelligence of our Heart—the Heart is the sacred portal.

Our Heart must be the North Star in all we do, as only our Heart truly knows what's of true effervescent beauty, health, art, grace, love, and magnanimity.

We all can manifest our own dreams and desires, and Lord only knows I wish for you to realize yours. There's truly no good or bad, spiritual or shallow, or whatever judgment you wish to attach to any dream or desire for a lived experience you want to manifest into your life.

But, do so Soulfully - literally, full of Soul - and don't make the mistake I once made and sell or lose your Soul in the process.

When we humans disconnect from our Heart, which is to say our Soul or spark of Divinity, no amount of "things" we can gain and accumulate in the Outer World will ever fill the void in our Inner World left by going soulless.

Our Heart is our North Star, and we're simply incapable of intentionally harming others when we stay connected and truly

express our Soul upon the canvas of all of Creation.

So, while it might seem like I am entirely focused on teaching mastery on the level of Mind in this course, please note the only reason I teach these concepts this way is because at the end of the day, this is a manifesting mastery course, not a course in spiritual purification.

Yet, I invite you—plead even—that you choose to use your Mind as I will teach you but follow your Heart at all times.

Good and beautiful things happen for you and the world around you when the Heart is our master, and the Mind its loyal servant.

And, as the Spiritual Poet we each are, what are we each here to do but to create and add our most beautiful art unto the canvas of all of Creation.

I see you and the view is magnificent.

JOURNAL + NOTES

Key chapter takeaways

_____

_____

_____

_____

_____

_____

_____

My growth opportunities - "the Gaps"

_____

_____

_____

_____

_____

_____

_____

Course Chapters

LOVE+
TRUTH™

CHAPTER

01

OWNERSHIP

THE JOURNEY FROM

Victimhood to Accountability

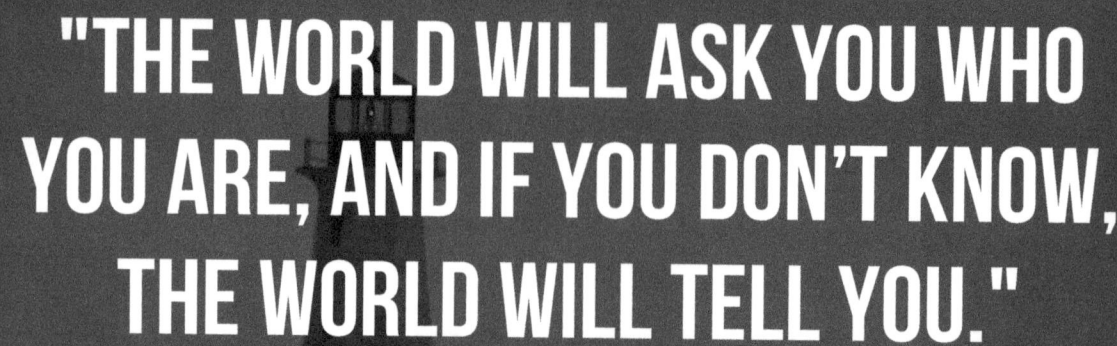

"THE WORLD WILL ASK YOU WHO YOU ARE, AND IF YOU DON'T KNOW, THE WORLD WILL TELL YOU."

- C.G. Jung -

MACRO PRINCIPLE

"

Hurricanes don't count.

―――――

You either shape and co-create your Destiny or the world will do it for you.

―――――

Your Power is in owning everything in your Life.

77

TEACHING

Forget Fairness.

Fairness is not a principle the Universe recognizes, operates by, or for that matter cares much about. This is not because the Universe is not just or not always in perfect order, but it's simply because "fairness" is an imaginary mental construct in our own limited perception of reality.

What you deem "fair" another person might perceive as patently "unfair." Fairness is merely an opinion or relative Truth, it's never a an undeniable fact or absolute Truth and that's what the Universe goes by in terms of Universal laws and principles.

So, dwelling on fairness is not something that's particularly helpful to us, in fact it disempowers us in many ways and steers us straight into the state of victimhood.

Whenever we adopt any belief that the Outer World determines or has power over our destiny, we have succumbed to a state of victimhood and disempowered ourselves entirely from being the Creator of our own destiny.

Additionally, within the state of victimhood is the fallacy that the Outer World dictates and controls what resides in our Inner World.

Nothing could be further from the Truth. Our Inner World—our perceptions, thoughts, feelings, and overall state—are our exclusive dominion and Kingdom to rule over.

We always have a choice as we are the guardian, gardener, steward, sculptor, and deity that governs our own Inner World.

Of course, victimhood is the choice —whether made consciously or unconsciously—to abdicate our choice to be the benevolent ruler of our Inner World. Either way, it's a choice we make even though for most victimhood is something the world erroneously taught them.

The Lure of Victimhood.

To become free of anything— whether that's an addiction like alcohol or cigarettes or an aspect of ourselves that no longer serves us—it's typically very helpful to understand what we are "gaining" from what we desire to liberate

78

ourselves from. That might sound contradictory, but generally speaking humans are driven by two core intrinsic drivers—we do or avoid things because we (a) gain something "desirable" from it; or (b) avoid something "painful" from it. And, sometimes it's a combination of both of these.

So, what might we "gain" or "avoid" from the state of victimhood?

A major lure and seduction of victimhood is that it's not our fault, we're not responsible, and can't be held accountable. Within all of this, we now have a legitimate excuse (so we believe) to bypass the things we should and could be doing to change our circumstances.

And, these things we should or could be doing are typically more difficult, challenging, and scary than remaining in the custodianship of our inner narrative of victimhood.

The fact is to learn, grow, evolve, expand, and rise into a new and better version of ourselves takes effort, courage, fortitude, and initiative on our part—at times copious amounts of all of those together and at the same time—but that's the only way to break free and liberate ourselves from "that" which we want to rise above.

Victimhood as your nemesis and

adversary has two mighty weapons in its arsenal and those are comfort and the known. Not only that, victimhood is a cunning manipulator of your inner dialogue if you allow it to orate freely and without censorship. It will be incessantly play the same record and somehow weave comfort and the known into its self-defeating narrative.

Don't allow victimhood access to the microphone and start embracing—loving even if you can—discomfort and the unknown as tell-tale signs and mile markers you can navigate by that you're on the path of change and transcendence to a new and better version of yourself.

Undoubtedly, fear, worry, doubt, and perhaps even anxiety will show up—simply let them be there and keep going anyway.

Everything that's known to you today, was at some point unknown and likely scary or intimidating to you. This is simply how our Mind deals with the unknown until this unknown becomes the known and the Mind drops its defenses.

The Power of Accountability.

The antidote to all forms or expressions of victimhood is accountability. The more absolute and resolute we step into accountability, the more potent the tonic that cleanses out all mental parasites that victimhood seeded in our expression of Being. All disempowering thoughts and beliefs, all habits that don't serve us, and all ideologies we've adapted that we're weak, feeble, incapable, or somehow not enough will start to be cleansed and removed from our Being when we fully step into accountability.

It's that potent and powerful, but at the same time there are no short cuts. Failing is fine, but then we get back on the horse right away as that's accountability also.

Signs we're making progress in accountability.

The beauty with radical accountability is that it changes our mental landscape and our Outer World experiences and circumstances very quickly.

When we fully and unapologetically step into radical accountability, we almost immediately start "seeing" where our Egoic Mind wants to negotiate, and it does so in covert ways such as offering up plausible sounding excuses or "just this one time" sort of inner dialogue bait.

If you choose to see and frame it this way, the Egoic Mind is making this a very easy game to gain the upper hand in which is why the downstream positive effects of tangible progress and inner growth can come so quickly if and when we

unequivocally decide to step into radical accountability. And, this is a "game" between you and you—I or anyone else can only show you how the game is played and what will make you successful in stepping into owning this Inner World game.

The Sanctum of Ownership.

All the qualities of Being we'll cover in this course are equally valuable and important in their own right, but there is an intention behind making Ownership the first quality of Being of this course.

Ownership is a "keystone" quality of Being when it comes to Manifesting Mastery—without Ownership even seeing yourself through this course becomes an almost insurmountable task.

To step into our full Powers as the Creator of our destiny, we must first and foremost step into Ownership through taking on radical accountability for our entire expression into Life itself.

We're both the sculpture and the sculptor, but without Ownership the elements around us will be doing most if not all of the sculpting.

Ownership then is this pivotal first choice—which is a decision—to become the sculptor of our own Life. Yes, I am inviting you to become the Michelangelo of your own Life and nothing less.

KEY LESSON

QUALITY OF BEING

Ownership

POISON

Victimhood

ANTIDOTE

Accountability

ACTION

1) Ownership is a decision

Are you ready, willing, and able to make a firm decision to commit yourself to "I Am Accountable"?

☐ **Yes, I commit wholeheartedly.**

☐ **No, I am not ready.**

2) Get clear about your "Why"

From the perspective of self-love, write a brief note from you to you "why" your answer above is true for you in this moment—your "why" is what will motivate and drive you to take aligned action.

Note: "No" is also a perfectly valid answer if that what's true for you right now.

_____

_____

_____

_____

_____

_____

_____

_____

_____

_____

_____

LOVE+ TRUTH. | dōjō

JOURNAL + NOTES

Key chapter takeaways

My growth opportunities - "the Gaps"

My next level aspiration - "the What"

My next level do's - "the How"

Notes

LOVE+ TRUTH. | dōjō

LIVE/VIDEO LESSON

CHAPTER

CLARITY

THE JOURNEY FROM

Disorder to Discernment

"IF A MAN KNOWS NOT WHICH PORT
HE SAILS, NO WIND IS FAVORABLE."

- Seneca -

MACRO PRINCIPLE

"

Vision dictates your direction, so does blindness.

———

Fuzzy vision makes for arduous detours & long journeys.

———

Get clear about your North Star, then go there and only there.

TEACHING

Rudderless Rowing.

There are countless reasons why for so many people Life itself often feels like an arduous slug, hard work, and an exhausting journey.

I totally get it and I pass no judgment whatsoever; I've been there myself more times than I care to admit.

This chapter we'll dive deep into one of the reasons I have observed that troubles and derails many—lack of clarity and in worst cases no clarity at all.

Lack of clarity (or none at all) leads us to engage in rudderless rowing—we're "doing" a lot but aren't really going where we want to go or making little progress getting there.

The point of Life itself is not to be busy, or even do a lot, but to create the lived experiences we most desire with the least amount of effort. Where's the wisdom in being so busy in Life itself that we're too exhausted to make love with it?

This rudderless rowing is a disease of our modern Western lifestyle and the societal norms and values our world impresses on us. The System heralds the tireless worker bee, in fact it's one of the many ways it keeps us disconnected from what's truly valuable and important such as love, connection, rest, play, health, and feeling our inter-connectedness with Nature and the people and world around us.

In addition, rudderless rowing ensures the System that you must keep rowing—and not pause to think too hard about why—as you're not really going anywhere so you always feel you're not quite where you wish to be.

The Quicksand of Disorder.

Underneath rudderless rowing is always a form of disorder which then is reflected in a lack of clarity which is the rudderless aspect of the rowing we're tirelessly doing.

So, let's take a closer look at disorder so we can start to discern (no pun intended) the insidious sinkhole of quicksand it tends to be.

Sometimes it's helpful to analyze a

90

word to really get to the true meaning of it. The strongest matches for the synonyms of the word "disorder" tells us volumes: anarchy, confusion, disarray, disarrangement, disorganization, jumble, mess, muddle, shambles, and discombobulation are the main ones but there are more.

Clearly, if any of the above is our prevailing mental state then we're going to be creating some form of chaos in our lived experiences—it simply cannot be any other way.

Order begets order and chaos begets chaos.

All chaos truly is, is a pattern of disorganization and within this we cannot help but find ourselves wrestling with confusion, disarray, and discombobulation. Of course, there are all sorts of beautiful and profound creative innovations that can be born from chaos and so it has its place and time but the efficient realization or actualization of manifestations are not born from chaos, those come from order.

Hence, in terms of manifesting "that" which we desire into a lived experience, disorder is our nemesis and the poison we have to neutralize with an antidote.

Before we get to the antidote, let's define and frame out how disorder usually reveals itself as it concerns

Clarity which is the quality of Being we're rowing towards in this chapter.

More often than not, disorder shows up as some form of indecision whether we do that consciously or unconsciously. Indecision comes in many disguises like wavering, doubting, over-analyzing, and mental looping which is going around on the mental hamster wheel without ever getting off.

Here's a fact of Life itself we all know—you will never know all the facts and information and the timing will never "seem" quite right to your Mind whose main job it is to worry incessantly about your safety and security.

We must navigate through Life making decisions all the time based on imperfect information as nothing that pertains to the future is ever all known to us.

The point is to gain mastery in making the best decisions you can in the moment without any undue delay and to staying open we might have to tweak, adjust, and course correct along the way.

The art of Life then becomes to read the tea leaves and make these course corrections timely, but not any sooner or later. This is why it's an art, only practice makes perfect.

The Peace of Discernment.

Discernment is the acuity and wisdom to cut out all the noise, distractions, energy drains, and all else that is not of service to us.

Discernment is the razor-sharp surgical scalpel that carves out what's in alignment for us and what's not.

Simplicity is the transcendent manifestation steroid and fertilizer —nothing else comes even close.

A laser beam—which is merely focused light—can cut a steel beam, whereas the best dispersed light can do is illuminate the steel beam from the shadows.

The simplicity of Life itself created by the masterful application of discernment is like stepping into an oasis of peace and tranquility. I promise you, this oasis is where you want to revel in Life itself.

Now, that oasis won't create itself—you must create this for yourself, and we can only do so by vigilantly and unapologetically cutting the weeds out of our garden.

All the people, circumstances, habits, tendencies, distractions, addictions, or anything else that's not in alignment with what we desire to create as a lived experience needs to be cut and removed from our Life.

We do so lovingly yet decisively and methodologically, and we make this an ongoing process throughout our lives, or our oasis will over time become a garden overgrown with weeds again.

Our scalpel in this is discernment and our North Star in what is welcome and in alignment and what's not is radical self-love which is never selfish or inconsiderate as you Being less than you can be and robbing this Universe of your true genius helps nobody, least of all you.

The Power of Clarity.

If you've ever wondered why some people were able to do or accomplish this or that and why you seemingly struggle to make meaningful progress, then look no further than Clarity.

I guarantee you they had Clarity on where they were headed, and I promise you they didn't have all the answers of the "how" at first either.

But, their Clarity is what allowed them to focus and bundle their efforts, to persevere through the inevitable challenges along the way and to cut through the fog as they commanded the Universe to reveal the "how" to them.

The Truth is, if we know where we're going—we have Clarity—the port will actually find us.

92

KEY LESSON

QUALITY OF BEING

Clarity

POISON

Disorder

ANTIDOTE

Discernment

ACTION

1) Clarity is a decision

Are you ready, willing, and able to make a firm decision to commit yourself to "I Am Discerning"?

☐ **Yes, I commit wholeheartedly.**

☐ **No, I am not ready.**

2) Get clear about your "Why"

From the perspective of self-love, write a brief note from you to you "why" your answer above is true for you in this moment—your "why" is what will motivate and drive you to take aligned action.

Note: "No" is also a perfectly valid answer if that what's true for you right now.

_____

_____

_____

_____

_____

_____

_____

_____

_____

_____

_____

LOVE+ TRUTH | dōjō

JOURNAL + NOTES

Key chapter takeaways

My growth opportunities - "the Gaps"

My next level aspiration - "the What"

_____

_____

_____

My next level do's - "the How"

_____

_____

_____

_____

_____

_____

_____

_____

Notes

_____

_____

_____

_____

_____

_____

_____

LOVE+ TRUTH. | dōjō

LIVE/VIDEO LESSON

CHAPTER

03

COMMITMENT

THE JOURNEY FROM
Indecision to Tenacity

"THE MOMENT ONE COMMITS ONESELF, THEN PROVIDENCE MOVES TOO.

A WHOLE STREAM OF EVENTS ISSUES FROM THE DECISION.

RAISING IN ONE'S FAVOR ALL MANNER UNFORESEEN INCIDENTS AND MEETINGS AND MATERIAL ASSISTANCE, WHICH NO MAN COULD HAVE DREAMT WOULD HAVE COME HIS WAY."

- W.H. Murray -

MACRO PRINCIPLE

"

Every quality worth having is a muscle.

———

Untrained, it will go weak and into atrophy.

———

Continuously trained, it will strengthen, develop muscle memory until it becomes a habit.

TEACHING

Option Overload.

Until fairly recently considering humans have been around for c. 300,000 years, mankind was predominantly preoccupied with mere survival.

This started slowly changing since the days of the Renaissance (c. 1600s) but it's only in the last century or so that this has radically changed for most people.

In the first or developed world especially, the pendulum has swung to the other extreme and people are now inundated with option overload.

Infinite choices while we are each finite in terms of time, space, and resources no matter how rich you are.

We can fly to any corner of the world at a moment's notice, buy just about anything from Amazon and have it delivered tomorrow, and there are limitless TV channels, movies, or music we can access.

Most things have also now become

disposable or readily replaceable—we've even reduced romance and intimate connection to a swipe left or right option with infinite options being presented as long as you keep swiping away.

Here's the rub with all of this, the infinity of the Universe is simply inexhaustible so no matter how hard we try to cover them all, we will not be able to.

And, there's a real cost to trying too many options as quantity comes at the expense of quality whereas the tradeoff of more quality—i.e. depth of experience—is we must sacrifice some variety.

This is the conundrum of the modern man and woman, and while I am not going to preach what anyone else should do—I can tell from personal experience that there comes a time and place where what we hunker most for is depth of experience and at that point foregoing options is no longer a real sacrifice.

Inherent in Commitment—whether this is a love interest, mission,

athletic pursuit, career, business, health, or what have you—is foregoing other options.

There's a monumental peace of mind that can be merely acquired by accepting this Truth about Life itself.

This Universe is infinite, and we're simply not.

The Wrath of Indecision.

Once again, indecision rears its ugly head even though the context is slightly different as it relates to Commitment—let me explain.

The wrath of indecision in relation to Commitment is that it renders our Commitment weak and impotent. Indecision guts our Commitment from all its strength and fierceness and so it becomes wobbly, unstable, ambiguous, and fickle.

This is perhaps most clearly exemplified by the dance between the Feminine and Masculine in a love relationship (note: I am not saying between a Woman and a Man—I am talking energies here, not biology—you do you).

When the Masculine lacks tenacity in his Commitment—the Feminine will experience a visceral reaction to this indecisiveness. She will withdraw, close down, protect herself, and generally feel unsafe.

She will simply not open up to flower, blossom, and expand into her full magnificence and if this lack of Commitment endures, she will even go barren and eventually revolt.

Here's the true wisdom to extract from that example as it's intended to be read and understood metaphorically more so than literally.

Everything in this Universe that has creation and birth within it—no matter what it is—is Feminine in essence. The Masculine fertilizes the egg with its sperm, but the Feminine births it into existence.

Regardless of whether we're a biological man or woman, in the process of manifesting something into our Life, the Universe is the Feminine principle and we're the Masculine principle.

To fertilize her—i.e. the Universe— we must first make her receptive to receiving our fertilization and we open her up by a fierce tenacity in our Commitment. For her to flower, blossom, and yield the fruits we desire to harvest we have to do our part which is Commit fully and unconditionally.

We must leave indecision behind and step into a relentless tenacity so she can feel our Commitment in every fiber of every cell.

Now, whatever sage relationship advise you might draw from all of that is up to you, consider it a bonus if you do.

The Torque of Tenacity.

In physics, torque is a measure of force. In a car, raw horsepower determines the possible top speed, but torque is a measure of the power of the engine.

Within Commitment, we don't care so much for raw horsepower or top speed, what we're after is torque and endurance as that's what will see us through.

We don't care for the vanity or bragging rights of peak performance, what will help us stay the course and finish the race is staying power.

Within tenacity we can find such beautiful and invaluable qualities of grit, persistence, perseverance, and determination. We become steadfast in our resolve, and this is what allows us to rise above the inevitable challenges and setbacks we will encounter when we set sail into oceans we haven't sailed and navigated before.

And tenacity is not something any of us is necessarily born with; it's not an innate talent that some have and others simply don't. Some might have an easier time training this muscle, but we each have this

muscle and so each of us has it within themselves to train this muscle and render tenacity a quality that we have habitualized into the bedrock of how we choose to show up in Life no matter the circumstances.

The Leverage of Commitment.

One of the most effervescent aspects of Commitment is the huge leverage it brings into our Life—it's literally a super-power that, as the quote by W. H. Murray states, makes Providence move too.

Providence of course is "that" we can only point at as words cannot truly describe, let alone explain, the invisible hand of God or the Divine intervention it refers to. Yet, we can know it exists as we likely all do and we do have the power to activate Providence on our behalf and we do so through our Commitment.

Our job is to do—to the very best of our abilities—all that's within our control, within our means, and within our capabilities living here on the earthly realm.

The very act of true unwavering Commitment is what activates the leverage of the Universe conspiring in our favor, in manners we could have never foreseen.

Admittedly, there's a bit of faith in that, but mostly just Commitment.

KEY LESSON

QUALITY OF BEING

Commitment

———

POISON

Indecision

———

ANTIDOTE

Tenacity

ACTION

1) Commitment is a decision

Are you ready, willing, and able to make a firm decision to commit yourself to "I Am Tenacious"?

☐ **Yes, I commit wholeheartedly.**

☐ **No, I am not ready.**

2) Get clear about your "Why"

From the perspective of self-love, write a brief note from you to you "why" your answer above is true for you in this moment—your "why" is what will motivate and drive you to take aligned action.

Note: "No" is also a perfectly valid answer if that what's true for you right now.

_____

_____

_____

_____

_____

_____

_____

_____

_____

_____

_____

LOVE+
TRUTH. dōjō

JOURNAL + NOTES

Key chapter takeaways

My growth opportunities - "the Gaps"

My next level aspiration - "the What"

_____

_____

_____

My next level do's - "the How"

_____

_____

_____

_____

_____

_____

_____

Notes

_____

_____

_____

_____

_____

_____

_____

LOVE+ TRUTH | dōjō

LIVE/VIDEO LESSON

CHAPTER

INTEGRITY

THE JOURNEY FROM

Deceit to Honor

"THE SUPERIOR MAN KNOWS WHAT'S RIGHT, THE INFERIOR MAN KNOWS WHAT SELLS."

- Confucius -

MACRO PRINCIPLE

"

Everything is simple, just not always easy.

Our Mind is often not trustworthy, our Heart always is.

Follow your Heart, beware the lure of comfort & expediency.

TEACHING

White Lies Everywhere.

Despite our Divine origins, here in our human avatar on the Earthly realm we're programmed and hardwired to be social animals and part of that is that we each want to be accepted and welcomed in.

Rejection and abandonment don't feel good, and there's even ancestral wounds that inform us it's unsafe as even just a few centuries ago being rejected from the tribe was essentially a death sentence.

In this context, white lies make sense and could even be seen as a logical and legitimate survival strategy—they are on some level and yet we're confronted once again with the paradoxical nature of Life itself once we explore this topic on the level of the spiritual realm.

Because white lies are still Falsehoods no matter how cutely we disguise them in plausible reasons and explanations. A lie is still a lie, no matter if we call it white or think we're doing some perceived "good" in the process.

For this course the white lies we

express into existence to not offend or harm others are not of the greatest concern. Even though, you will likely find you'll pause more and pause as you move deeper into the embodiment of Integrity until you'll hardly ever utter them again —this purification process will unfold organically so no we don't need to spend more time of this variety of white lies.

The ones we're concerned with for this course are the white lies you tell yourself to not hurt or harm your own Ego.

Yep, maybe read that again as this is an important point. The white lies we tell ourselves are insidious and make for festering wounds as they cover up what we lack the courage and fortitude to face head on.

The deceit within these white lies we tell ourselves is what blocks us from the bitter tonic we should be swallowing to cleanse out these festering wounds.

Why?

Because these wounds we each have—and then cover up with white

114

lies—are misperceptions about ourselves or Life itself which then become our blind spots preventing us from seeing what's truly available for us.

By definition, a blind spot is not what we in theory cannot see, it's always what we are unwilling to see.

Of course, white lies and the blind spots they cover is but a small part of deceit so let's go deeper.

The Disease called Deceit.

The world-at-large looks and operates the way it does largely because of the prevalence of deceit in all its forms and expressions.

Dishonesty, corruption, fraud, malfeasance, self-dealing, and a blatant disregard for all others (including Mother Earth) is now pervasive throughout our political, government, judicial, educational, corporate, and financial institutions —they're all infected with and by this Anti-Life virus.

When the institutions of society get infected, it's inevitable society and the populous itself does as well as there's no longer a fundamental Integrity to the fabric of society.

Deceit is a like a cancerous disease and unless confronted with the medicine called honor the cancer will spread until such time it

mortally wounds the organism that gives it Life in the first place.

In this course, we're not concerned with the "macro" which is our society-at-large, but all phenomena in this Universe operate in the "micro" as they do in the "macro."

And, so we can take all I said before and equally apply this to the micro —our individual Life—and observe deceit works and operates in the very same way.

Deceit is also a slippery slope, it always starts small with some innocuous little deceit like a white lie and then before you know it we're into bigger deceits like cheating a little on our tax return, cutting a corner on something, and before you know it we're blatantly dishonest about something to our partner or employer or what have you. The point is, deceit will inevitably creep into most, if not all, areas of your Life if you allow it to exist at all.

I could layer in all the Karmic repercussions as well, but I don't want to tread into ideologies of sin, guilt, and shame (as those are rooted in religious ideas of morality, not spiritual principles).

What I am more interested in conveying is how deceit disharmonizes the equilibrium of Life itself which then has to be compensated for as the Universe is always and all times harmonizing itself back to a state of perfect equilibrium of wholeness.

And, wholeness is actually the state of Integrity as for something to be in Integrity it means that it is undivided and whole.

The opposite of whole and undivided is broken and divided—see what I was pointing at now when I spoke of the state of the world today?

The Ethos of Honor.

Deceit doesn't feel good. Our Egoic Mind might talk it straight and justify the deceit in all sorts of seemingly clever yet ultimately disingenuous ways, but deep down we know better.

We know we violated something, even when we can't quite put our finger on it—what we in fact violated is our own Soul which is directly connected with the totality of this entire Universe.

We, through our Egoic Mind, might lose our connection with this totality but our Soul never does. Our Soul knows and it feels every single ripple effect that goes into this Universe through our every thought, word, and action. When this ripple effect is one of deceit, our Soul knows it disturbed the "Force" as they say in Star Wars.

Honor is the antidote and pathway to step into an embodiment of Integrity. Within honor we find such qualities as virtue, respect, decency, reverence, dignity, nobility, love, truth, honesty, sincerity, justice and fairness.

These effervescent qualities—when embodied and expressed—are like a medicinal balm that promote and procure harmony within ourselves and all else we touch in Life.

Nobody will ever accuse you of Being too honorable for their liking—even the most crooked and lost Souls are magnetized to those who can be a flagbearer of honor as it's a excruciatingly high standard.

The Profits of Integrity.

Of all the qualities of Being covered in this course, the profits of Integrity might very well bring you the greatest true riches—which are invariably all those that money can't buy.

Integrity is the great harmonizer of Life itself as it's the Order that brings everything into wholeness, and on the micro-level of your individual Life this will inevitably reveal itself as "smooth sailing."

When we're in true harmony with ourselves and all there is, we remove friction and with less friction things get smooth and agreeable—we also call this grace.

116   LOVE+TRUTH. | dōjō

KEY LESSON

QUALITY OF BEING
Integrity

———

POISON
Deceit

———

ANTIDOTE
Honor

ACTION

1) Integrity is a decision

Are you ready, willing, and able to make a firm decision to commit yourself to " I Am Honorable"?

☐ **Yes, I commit wholeheartedly.**

☐ **No, I am not ready.**

2) Get clear about your "Why"

From the perspective of self-love, write a brief note from you to you "why" your answer above is true for you in this moment—your "why" is what will motivate and drive you to take aligned action.

Note: "No" is also a perfectly valid answer if that what's true for you right now.

_____

_____

_____

_____

_____

_____

_____

_____

_____

_____

_____

LOVE+ TRUTH | dōjō

JOURNAL + NOTES

Key chapter takeaways

My growth opportunities - "the Gaps"

My next level aspiration - "the What"

_____

_____

_____

My next level do's - "the How"

_____

_____

_____

_____

_____

_____

_____

_____

Notes

_____

_____

_____

_____

_____

_____

_____

_____

_____

LOVE+ TRUTH. | dōjō

LIVE/VIDEO LESSON

CHAPTER

DISCIPLINE

THE JOURNEY FROM
Sloth to Vigor

"THROUGH DISCIPLINE COMES FREEDOM."

- Aristotle -

124

MACRO PRINCIPLE

"

Every great thing is still just made up of tiny atoms.

———

The way you do anything, is the way you do everything.

———

Honor the small steps, and the big leaps will inevitably follow.

TEACHING

Slackers Slack.

Nobody has ever slacked or slothed their way to great heights or new pinnacles whether in the material or spiritual realm.

We can certainly masterfully take advantage of the Law of Least Effort, but this law and sloth are two very different animals.

The fact is slackers slack, and slackers tend to make very little progress or advancements in Life other than whatever falls accidently into their lap. And, again, I am not just referring to the trophies, fame, fortune, and applause our world is preoccupied with. This principle of Life applies equally to everything like love relationships and marriages, friendships, raising a child, learning to play an instrument or new sport, cooking, carpentry, and just about anything else but especially ripening in spiritual maturity and wisdom.

Realizing growth in the spiritual realm is the ultimate endeavor where sloth will get you nowhere.

So, let's see what sloth really entails

as I realize some of you might not be that familiar with this somewhat uncommon word.

The dictionary defines sloth as laziness, listlessness, idleness, inactivity, inertia, indolence, laxness, lethargy, and sluggishness.

From that list it's glaringly obvious that within sloth we have entered a state of general paralysis towards engaging with Life itself—and we know from the self-study part that unless we change, nothing really changes.

So, sloth then is the surefire method by which we get stuck in the purgatory of our current circumstances and lived experiences. Groundhog Day on endless repeat basically.

Sloth also tends to reflect in all areas of our Life as the maxim "the way we do anything, is the way we do anything" fails to be accurate very rarely.

So, chances are that if your car is a mess, your closet is a mess, your bed is a mess, and your desk is a mess than more likely than not

it's predictable that your kitchen is a mess also and so are your finances, credit score, career, relationships, etc.

Maybe you're a unicorn where this maxim doesn't apply, but odds are it does. Sure, maybe there are gradations and nuances, and some areas of your Life are less "slothy" than others. Still, there's a very good reason why all ancient wisdom traditions have some ethos, principle, or commandment that speaks to the detriments of sloth and uncleanliness—as it gets us stuck, stale, and barren in Life and arid soils can host no plants that bear plentiful fruits.

Pride in Doing Things Well.

I had a spiritual mentor tell me once: "Unless your spirituality changes the way you do the dishes, you haven't advanced much yet."

I was really puzzled by that statement at first as I didn't see an obvious connection between spirituality and a menial task as doing the dishes. I also didn't have a Discipline problem, I fortunately never had as I was blessed with a natural proclivity towards self-discipline and whatever I lacked my parents drilled into me from an early age.

The "answer" hit me later when we discussed doing all tasks well or don't do them at all. The answer to

the riddle is where we place our awareness in the moment. To do any job or task well—no matter how insignificant or menial—requires we bring our awareness into it and wherever we place our awareness we now have a choice to do it well.

Any job or task we do with less than our full awareness, is a job or task we're doing mechanically on autopilot and that will always show in the results. To put our true effort, care, skill, genius, and love into anything, we must give it our full awareness.

Sloth is the equivalent to putting no awareness into anything we do, we're running Life on the bare minimum pilot light.

Conversely, vigor is bringing our full awareness into something and the intensity of focus that creates is what literally invigorates—energizes —that which we're doing.

Whatever we energize in Life comes alive—it's as if we infuse it with our own Life Force.

This is the power of bringing a sense of vigor into each and every area of our Life and what it organically cultivates is Discipline but more on that later.

Vigor is a highly valuable trait that we can cultivate simply by routine application—there's no special trick, code, or inborn talent we need to adopt vigor into our Life expression or Beingness.

It's simply a choice we make. We decide to be vigorous in all we do, it's that simple.

The investment of effort and little bit of willpower to overcome the initial resistance of our Mind to release its "slothy" ways is richly rewarded with almost instantaneous dividends—change happens very fast when we transmute our sloth into vigor and in many cases the results are tangible and directly observable.

Vigor also lends itself well to start in small and manageable ways and then once we have gained some momentum, we can let this momentum do the heavy lifting for us as we expand the areas of our Life where vigor governs.

So, by all means go all in with vigor but at the same time it's okay to take something bite-size for you and start there. The point is to start and start right away.

The Might of Discipline.

Discipline is a powerful engine which once purring along has the capacity to create radical freedom.

Many people find it challenging to see how Discipline—which to them appears the antithesis of freedom—

can be the very thing that unlocks freedom.

Here's how that works: Discipline within it very application breeds and promotes efficiency, expediency, and least effort.

What we do with vigor as a matter of Discipline, we tend to become highly proficient and efficient at—this happens all organically as we simply pursue things with vigor.

All time wasted in procrastination, delays, stalling, or doing jobs and tasks subpar which then require us to correct or redo them is time we now regain through Discipline.

There's no more freedom than having more free time while all that needs to be done has been done well.

And, and that's just linear time. We also free up our mental bandwidth as Discipline is efficient and with vigor we become good and expedient at getting the tasks of Life done with minimal mental strain —freeing up mental bandwidth means we have more time to imagine, dream, create, or just relax and enjoy the equanimity of a Mind at peace.

Discipline is a doorway, and while not usually seen in that light, it might very well be one of the most spiritual doorways you'll ever cross.

LOVE+ TRUTH. | dōjō

KEY LESSON

QUALITY OF BEING
Discipline

POISON
Sloth

ANTIDOTE
Vigor

ACTION

1) Discipline is a decision

Are you ready, willing, and able to make a firm decision to commit yourself to "I Am Vigorous"?

☐ **Yes, I commit wholeheartedly.**

☐ **No, I am not ready.**

2) Get clear about your "Why"

From the perspective of self-love, write a brief note from you to you "why" your answer above is true for you in this moment—your "why" is what will motivate and drive you to take aligned action.

Note: "No" is also a perfectly valid answer if that what's true for you right now.

_____

_____

_____

_____

_____

_____

_____

_____

_____

_____

LOVE+ TRUTH. | dōjō

JOURNAL + NOTES

Key chapter takeaways

My growth opportunities - "the Gaps"

My next level aspiration - "the What"

_____

_____

_____

My next level do's - "the How"

_____

_____

_____

_____

_____

_____

_____

Notes

_____

_____

_____

_____

_____

_____

_____

LOVE+ TRUTH | dōjō

LIVE/VIDEO LESSON

CHAPTER

06

CONCENTRATION

THE JOURNEY FROM
Disorganization to Focus

"CONCENTRATE ALL YOUR THOUGHTS UPON THE WORK AT HAND - THE SUN'S RAYS DO NOT BURN UNTIL BROUGHT TO A FOCUS."

- Alexander Graham Bell -

MACRO PRINCIPLE

"

Even the Sun's rays diffuse in Power as they scatter.

———

Distraction & chaos suspends dreams.

———

Order self-organizes once put in motion, but we must command this Super Power.

TEACHING

Distraction Abound.

Show me unfinished, incomplete, or subpar quality work and I will show you a lack of Concentration had something to do with it.

On the material plane of Mother Earth, we have to see things through to harvest the fruits grown from the seeds we sowed.

We also have to tend to the garden or our lands to see to it that the seeds sprout and then grow.

Distraction in all its many forms is the dissipation of Concentration— and dissipation is the process of disorganizing or things coming undone.

In our modern-day world there are an infinite number of distractions pulling at us each and every moment, and as mentioned earlier the System designed it this way on purpose as that serves its larger agenda.

The System wants and needs the populous to serve in two distinct capacities: (a) as indentured worker bees; and (b) as insatiable

consumers—there's no grand conspiracy theory behind this as this is simply the natural consequence of an economic system that is designed to perpetuate growth and a return on capital invested.

To do so, you simply need the general populous to work and produce goods and services and also consume precipitously so the supply and demand side remain in equilibrium. The compound growth is then created by creating debt which has the added benefit of indebtedness which is a highly effective way to keep the populous on the hamster wheel.

I explain the above as the System actively promotes endless distractions where Las Vegas is merely a microcosm of the macrocosm.

The System wants and needs you to follow celebrities, influencers, and get lost into such nebulous things as the latest fashion, hit shows, and must-have new products and services. It needs you to be so blinded by image and status that paying $1,300 for a

LOVE+ TRUTH | dōjō

Gucci handbag that cost maybe $40 to make, makes total sense to you.

Alcohol, marijuana, sugary foods, painkillers, anti-depressants, etc. are also all promoted and advertised as they numb us and sink us deeper into sleepwalking through Life.

Distraction is the bottomless sinkhole of escapism where we remain perhaps superficially and seemingly functional by society's skewed standards, yet our true genius is never activated and brought into expression on the canvas of all of Creation.

Disorganization Unpacked.

The venom of disorganization is that it cannot lead to anything but disarray and then inevitably some gradation of Chaos.

Whereas Order has the effect of unifying, binding, fusing, and amalgamating matter(s), Chaos has the very opposite effect.

The process of manifestation of "that" which exists as a potentiality —i.e. idea, dream, imagination—in the ethereal or non-physical realm into something of form, substance, or matter in the material or physical realm requires there to be a self-organizing power.

This self-organizing power in our

Universe is Order. Order is what commands the infinite intelligence within consciousness to organize itself so it can transmute itself from the unmanifest into the manifest which we recognize here on the material realm as anything of form, substance, or matter.

Incidentally, this includes "that" which we experience as a relationship of any kind even though that has no physical form or structure.

We can know this to be true as we can each recognize a relationship because it contains the energetic structure of the material realm.

In fact, even though the way it's described here might be new to you, the understanding of these principles is self-evident as we each know intuitively a factory cannot produce finished products of any quality when it operates in a state of disorganization. Relationships falter and inevitably fail when chaos and disorganization govern and so forth.

Life itself is a very different lived experience when we "have our sh*t together" and when we don't—this isn't rocket-science yet we might encounter some resistance from our Mind which likes to argue Order comes at the expense of our creativity and spontaneity so for the sake of completion let's also debunk that myth here. This myth is premised on the notion that the wellspring of creativity and imagination is Chaos and not Order.

The disconnect here is that the fundamental reality—that which we can call the Infinite Field of Consciousness (or God, Creator, Monad, Brahman, Great Spirit, Infinite Intelligence, Quantum Field or whatever label you prefer)—is premised on infinite and eternal Order.

Chaos, when it arises, is akin to the choppy waters and blistery storms on the surface layers of the ocean yet the deepest oceanic trenches are always calm and undisturbed.

Hence, what we see and recognize as Chaos is just a microcosm of what's ultimately rooted in infinite Order—this is where the axiom "the seed of Order is always nested within Chaos" comes from where "nested" implies within the core or heart of it.

The Force of Focus.

Focus is our great ally as it's the centrifugal force that unifies otherwise disparate or scattered energy.

When we focus our energy which always starts with fixating our awareness on some "thing" we start to command the Universe to move Providence and come to our aid in all manners unforeseen.

Focus activates, unlocks, and galvanizes within us the drive, inspiration, and willpower to build momentum. Momentum is what enables the flapping of a butterfly's wing on one continent to build into a hurricane that comes ashore in another.

Without focus there can be no Concentration, and without Concentration there cannot be the activation of the self-organizing principles that transmute the unmanifest into the manifest—it's just that simple.

The Yielding of Concentration.

While "yield" within the word "yielding" refers to profit, crop, or interest; yielding refers to the process of accommodating or making way for something.

The Universe invariably yields to Concentration through the process of concurrence or amalgamation—a desire or wish energetically amplified through Concentration will inevitably come together as in being fused into existence.

This is the inherent power within Concentration and the higher the amplitude of Concentration we can hold for extended periods of time, the easier it becomes to manifest that which we desire or wish for as a lived experience.

So, this is why to focus on Concentration (pun intended).

140

KEY LESSON

QUALITY OF BEING

Concentration

———

POISON

Disorganization

———

ANTIDOTE

Focus

ACTION

1) Concentration is a decision

Are you ready, willing, and able to make a firm decision to commit yourself to "I Am Focused"?

☐ **Yes, I commit wholeheartedly.**

☐ **No, I am not ready.**

2) Get clear about your "Why"

From the perspective of self-love, write a brief note from you to you "why" your answer above is true for you in this moment—your "why" is what will motivate and drive you to take aligned action.

Note: "No" is also a perfectly valid answer if that what's true for you right now.

_____

_____

_____

_____

_____

_____

_____

_____

_____

_____

_____

LOVE+ TRUTH | dōjō

JOURNAL + NOTES

Key chapter takeaways

_____
_____
_____
_____
_____
_____
_____
_____

My growth opportunities - "the Gaps"

_____
_____
_____
_____
_____
_____
_____
_____

My next level aspiration - "the What"

_____

_____

_____

My next level do's - "the How"

_____

_____

_____

_____

_____

_____

_____

Notes

_____

_____

_____

_____

_____

_____

_____

LOVE+ TRUTH. | dōjō

LIVE/VIDEO LESSON

CHAPTER

07

FORTITUDE

THE JOURNEY FROM
Softness to Grit

"PATIENCE AND FORTITUDE CONQUER ALL THINGS."

- Ralph Waldo Emerson -

MACRO PRINCIPLE

66

Grit is a choice we make, not an ability we're born with.

———

Soft healers make festering wounds.

———

There are no real external obstacles, only illusionary internal ones.

TEACHING

Weak, Soft, and Sickly.

There's absolutely nothing wrong with failing—even when we fail time and again in miserable ways—as failing is part and parcel of the process of endeavoring and venturing into new things.

But, stopping short or simply giving up when the going gets tough is not the same as failing—it's capitulating to the Outer World circumstances we perceive to be bigger and mightier than us.

Of course, there's a very fine line there as sometimes the wisest decision we can make is to surrender to the circumstances and abort mission—the nuance is in discerning whether the "problem" is in climbing the mountain or the mountain we're climbing.

If the problem is the latter—there's zero failure in concluding we picked the wrong mountain to climb.

If the problem is the climbing of the mountain, then we have entered the phase of the journey where the wheat gets separated from the chaff. This is where our mettle gets

tested and then forged if we have the Fortitude to see ourselves through this phase which is merely a form of initiation into a better, stronger, and more resilient version of ourselves.

Our world—again the System—actually prefers you to stay weak, soft, and mildly sickly as that way you're far more controllable and gullible to the infinite variety of escapism on offer.

The world doesn't want you too strong and independent as that in and by itself is an act of rebellion against the System which prefers all its minions to be docile, compliant, and subservient to the System.

This is just a matter of economics and how to best leverage and utilize the productive assets and resources of the economy of which human capital is just one of the main inputs alongside natural capital.

The only real point to take away from all this is not to look at the world to teach or show you how to escape being weak, soft, and sickly —it won't as it has no vested

LOVE+ TRUTH | dōjō

interest in doing so. Instead, the world will provide you with endless pacifiers to keep you comfortable and domesticated to the System—again, this is simply in its economic interest.

The Subtle Slide into Softness.

For those that have awakened and embarked on the spiritual path, there's more often than not a subtle slide into softness.

Within our spiritual awakening, our Heart opens up and since the Heart is the citadel of our Feminine intelligence this typically coincides with a release of Feminine energy which before was imprisoned in our closed off Heart. As this liberated Feminine energy permeates our entire human avatar, there's a period of time where we have to learn to dance with the distinct energetic tonality of this liberated Feminine energy—this is especially true for men who are naturally Masculine-energy dominant but also for many women as the world taught and forced them to lean heavily into their Masculine energy to compete for worldly success and social recognition in the "game Man plays."

It's like the pendulum swings to the other extreme before it harmonizes into a healthy equilibrium state. So, as we awaken spiritually, there's a loosening or detachment that occurs from the material world as

this new and exhilarating spiritual world just opened up for us. All the things in the material world—including the "game Man plays"—lose their vice grip on us. Suddenly, all these material world matters and priorities lose some of their importance and within that our interest in those pursuits organically wanes. We then naturally make this subtle slide into softness as we simply aren't as motivated or inspired any longer by the things that used to be of the utmost importance to us.

All of this is a natural part of the awakening process and although each individual might experience this in slightly different ways; broad strokes all people that awaken move through this phase in one way or another.

So far, so good. Yet, this is supposed to be a temporary phase and when we get lost indefinitely in the spiritual realm and resist integrating our existence in the material realm with our newfound spiritual realm, we tend to drift into the realm of spiritual bypassing.

We're multi-dimensional beings and while here on Earth in a human avatar these two dimensions—the earthly and the spiritual—are intended to be harmonized so we're both grounded in the material realm while still strongly connected with the spiritual realm. This is actually where the rubber meets the road and true spiritual maturity is mastered as the "point" is to live spiritually connected in the material world.

And in the material world, if we want to gain mastery in manifesting our dreams and desires, requires copious amounts of Fortitude as we're going to need perseverance, resilience, strength, and courage to transmute the unmanifest into the manifest as a lived experience.

There's also such a "thing" as spiritual Fortitude but that pertains to courageously navigating the pathless land of the spiritual realms so that's outside the scope of this course.

The Essence of Grit.

Grit is pure poetry of the human spirit—we all have access to it, recognize it immediately in others, and we all know deep down it moves mountains and wins battles.

Within grit we find strength of character, resolve, and what we colloquially call "backbone."

Grit is our ability to bear down and grind it out, to see ourselves through and past the obstacles on our path with steadfastness and a certain level of hardiness.

When we decide grit is the mettle of my character, Fortitude comes

online organically as if it's called into existence through the very presence of grit in our spirit.

Grit we can act on, cultivate, and commit to—Fortitude is more the product of grit put into action.

As with everything, it's always better to start small than to not start at all. So, if grit is something that needs some cultivation in you, start small in an area where you feel confident you can succeed and make small wins.

These small wins will start building momentum and before you know it grit has taken over the tenancy of the house where weakness was squatting before.

The Beatitude of Fortitude.

The one with Fortitude is blessed for she or he is ready built for realizing their dreams, desires, and aspirations.

No matter your level of spiritual advancement or purity, Life itself will invariably throw you curveballs, present you with obstacles and challenges, and put you to task no matter what you set your sights on.

That's simply the nature of Life itself, it's designed that way as in the wise words of Confucius: "the gem cannot be polished without friction nor man without trials."

152

KEY LESSON

QUALITY OF BEING

Fortitude

POISON

Softness

ANTIDOTE

Grit

ACTION

1) Fortitude is a decision

Are you ready, willing, and able to make a firm decision to commit yourself to "I Am Gritty"?

☐ **Yes, I commit wholeheartedly.**

☐ **No, I am not ready.**

2) Get clear about your "Why"

From the perspective of self-love, write a brief note from you to you "why" your answer above is true for you in this moment—your "why" is what will motivate and drive you to take aligned action.

Note: "No" is also a perfectly valid answer if that what's true for you right now.

_____

_____

_____

_____

_____

_____

_____

_____

_____

_____

LOVE+ TRUTH. | dōjō

JOURNAL + NOTES

Key chapter takeaways

My growth opportunities - "the Gaps"

My next level aspiration - "the What"

_____

_____

_____

My next level do's - "the How"

_____

_____

_____

_____

_____

_____

_____

_____

Notes

_____

_____

_____

_____

_____

_____

_____

LOVE+ TRUTH. | dōjō

LIVE/VIDEO LESSON

CHAPTER

08

RESILIENCE

THE JOURNEY FROM
Fragility to Agility

"NO MAN EVER STEPS IN THE SAME RIVER TWICE, FOR IT'S NOT THE SAME RIVER AND HE'S NOT THE SAME MAN."

- Heraclitus -

MACRO PRINCIPLE

"

Water can't break.

You cannot change the nature of Change itself, nor that Life itself is nothing but change.

Rigidity can only falter with time, fluidity adapts and adjusts and has Staying Power.

TEACHING

The Dishonesty in Fragility.

The Truth is, we are actually not fragile at all. If anything, we might be somewhat vulnerable physically as accidents can harm or kill us but we're simply not fragile.

In fact, we're really robust as no matter the illness, loss, harm done or even heartbreak, we have the inherent ability to rebound and move on with Life.

The weak link in all of this is our Egoic Mind—that's the only place where fragility truly lives when it rears its ugly head.

Only in our perception and thoughts can we be offended, beaten, and enslaved to matters belonging to the Outer World.

And, that's where the dishonesty resides—as our Inner World is our exclusive dominion and allowing anything in the Outer World to color the waters of our Inner World is acquiescing to the Falsehood that our Inner World is not our exclusive dominion.

Fragility then exists on the mental plane of beliefs, ideas, and thoughts which are all psychological constructs which means they're not real.

Not real in the sense as the great Stoic philosopher and Roman Emperor Marcus Aurelius put it: "Everything we hear is an opinion, not a fact. Everything we see is a perspective, not the Truth."

To undo, unwind, and release our mental fragility is a momentous step forward in liberating ourselves from the stranglehold of opinions and viewpoints held by others in our Outer World.

The Grace within Agility.

Agility is another one of those poetic qualities which enriches us with such attributes as nimbleness, dexterity, swiftness, cleverness, and suppleness just to name a few.

What is Life itself but a highly dynamic and ever-changing experience where the pieces on the chessboard are always moving about, the weather and seasons always change, and even all the people and circumstances are always changing if not for aging and everyone's inevitable expiration date called death.

LOVE+ TRUTH | dōjō

This is simply the nature of Life itself and agility allows us to be with all that change—and the more agility we master to bring into our Being, the more we can be with and move through Life with grace.

And within grace, we can always see a distinct texture of elegance, refinement, and wisdom.

Just bring someone to Mind you know personally that has this cloak of grace about them. You will not have to dig too deep to discern that underlying this grace this person has an agility about them as they navigate their way through Life.

At closer examination, you'll also find that this same person is not somehow miraculously spared from the typical hardships, problems, challenges, or obstacles all others encounter.

It's just that their grace—which has its origins in their agility—somehow seems to neutralize and filter out the typical drama, fireworks, and low points others wrestle with when confronted with similar situations and Life events.

All of this is because their agility makes them highly resilient. They flow and bend with Life where others stay rigid and break.

This sort of agility resides first and foremost on the mental plane in our Mind. The rigidity or agility in which we perceive the world dictates "how" we're able to be with the events and circumstances in our Outer World.

The more rigid the beliefs we hold about how the Outer World—inclusive of all people— "should" be and show up, the more the world will disappoint and break us.

That's not to say we should not have our own moral compass and North Star, but we use that merely to guide us in our own expression into and interaction with the world around us.

We don't impose this on the world as a "should"—if anything, we might hold it as an aspiration for the world-at-large and than welcome and celebrate it when we witness it.

What this sort of application of agility moves us toward is surrendering the need to judge everything around us and this liberates an enormous amount of mental bandwidth and energy.

The ability to just observe and witness, without feeling compelled to have an opinion or judge is a total game-changer in terms of cultivating endless amounts of resilience to whatever might be occurring in the world around us.

The Significance of Resilience.

The famed mythologist Joseph Campbell spoke often of the Power of Myth (it's also an interview series which I highly recommend) and he was also the one that coined the term "The Hero's Journey."

unless with have cultivated the Resilience to see ourselves through this sacred journey where the "Dark Night of the Soul" represents the Abyss of the journey.

Our Resilience then has an outsized

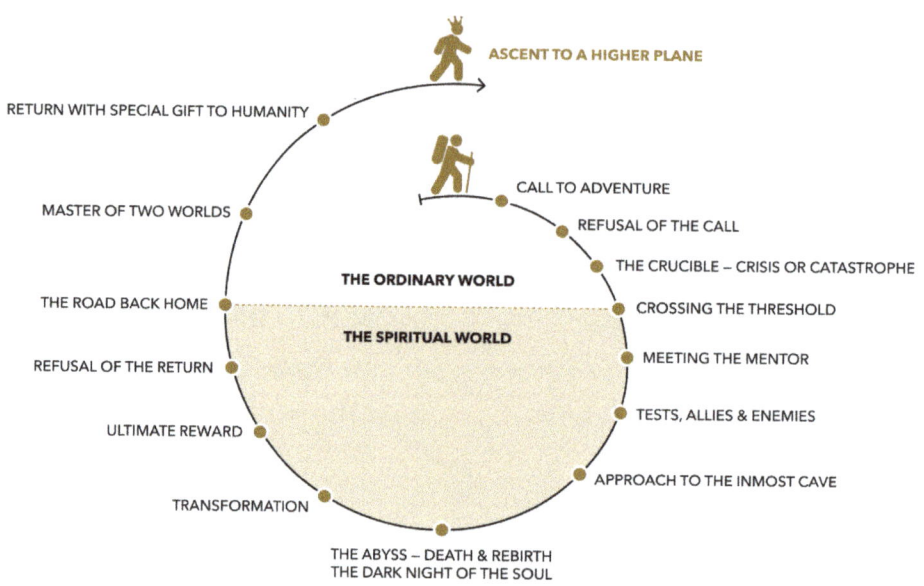

As Campbell explained, myths around the world and throughout history contain the archetypical blueprint of humanity—or in other words, the journey we must all travel to become self-realized.

We are each living our own Hero's Journey (see also illustration) and within this rite of passage to each higher plane of consciousness, we must pass through certain "stations" and complete the cycle only for the next cycle to next higher plane to emerge and so on and so forth.

Within this evolutionary path of mankind, we cannot progress

impact and significance on our ability to navigate our way through the peaks but especially the valleys of Life.

As a quality of character, we see Resilience always resurface within each hero in all fables and myths and this same storyline structure is what we can now see in our movies and films.

Resilience is what renders you the hero of your own journey, it's what you lean on when there's little else to grasp unto.

And, the beauty is, we all have it within us—no exceptions!

164

KEY LESSON

QUALITY OF BEING

Resilience

—

POISON

Fragility

—

ANTIDOTE

Agility

ACTION

1) Resilience is a decision

Are you ready, willing, and able to make a firm decision to commit yourself to "I Am Agile"?

☐ **Yes, I commit wholeheartedly.**

☐ **No, I am not ready.**

2) Get clear about your "Why"

From the perspective of self-love, write a brief note from you to you "why" your answer above is true for you in this moment—your "why" is what will motivate and drive you to take aligned action.

Note: "No" is also a perfectly valid answer if that what's true for you right now.

_____

_____

_____

_____

_____

_____

_____

_____

_____

_____

_____

LOVE+ TRUTH | dōjō

JOURNAL + NOTES

Key chapter takeaways

My growth opportunities - "the Gaps"

My next level aspiration - "the What"

_____

_____

_____

My next level do's - "the How"

_____

_____

_____

_____

_____

_____

_____

_____

Notes

_____

_____

_____

_____

_____

_____

_____

_____

LOVE+ TRUTH. | dōjō

LIVE/VIDEO LESSON

CHAPTER

09

MASTERY

THE JOURNEY FROM

Incompetence to Genius

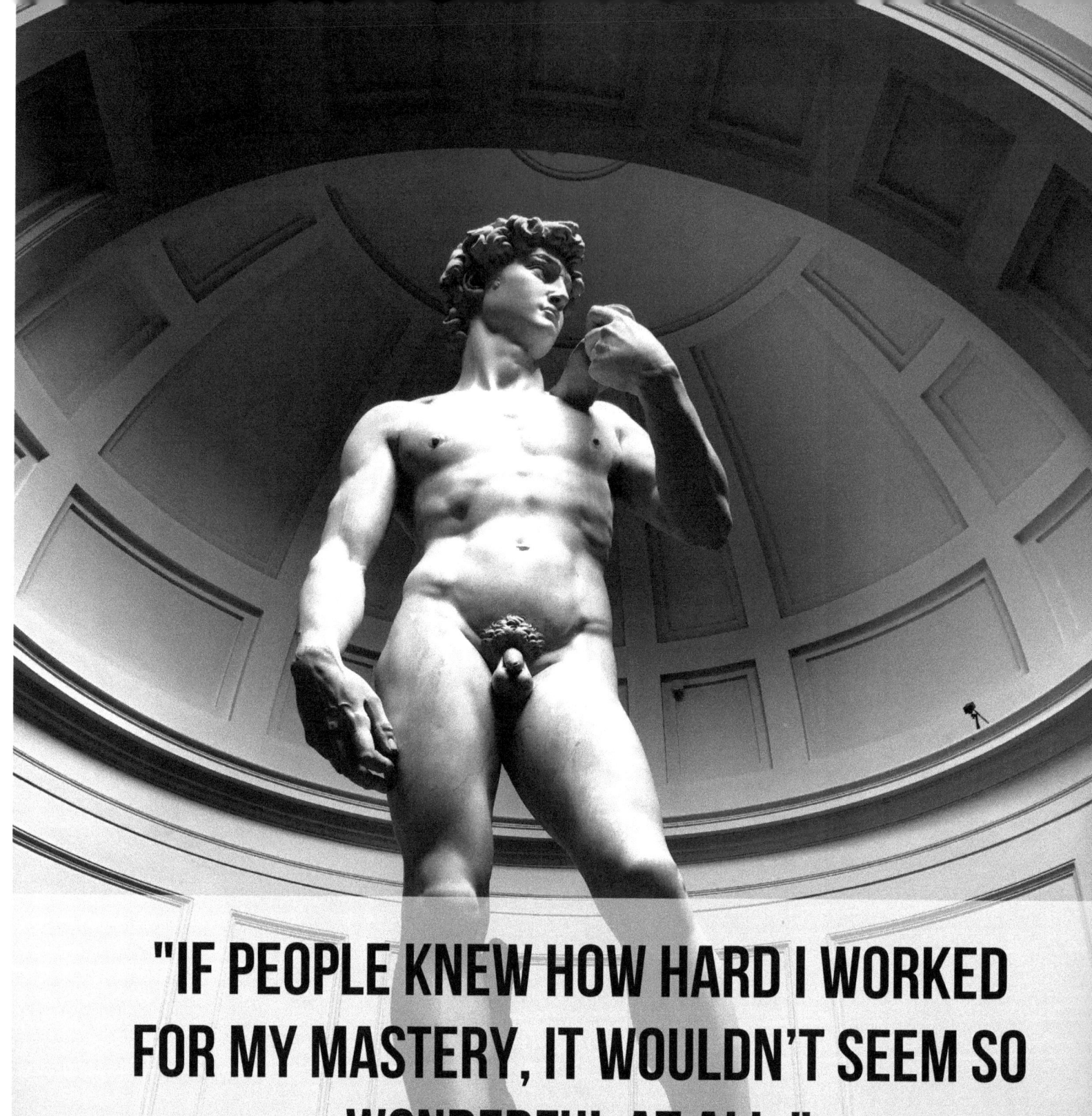

"IF PEOPLE KNEW HOW HARD I WORKED FOR MY MASTERY, IT WOULDN'T SEEM SO WONDERFUL AT ALL."

- Michelangelo -

MACRO PRINCIPLE

"

There's zero mystery to skill and capability.

———

Nobody arrives at the level of Genius by fluke or accident.

———

Only the seeds we fertilize grow to eventually flower and blossom.

TEACHING

Easy Street.

Malcolm Gladwell in his best-selling book "Outliers" quantified it takes a certain level of devoted dedication to any craft or skill to attain the level of mastery or genius—he phrased this the "10,000-hour rule" which has now become the de facto benchmark.

Later, other researchers and scientists went deeper into this popularized idea, and some concluded the 10,000 hours is really 100 hours of intellectual learning and 9,900 hours of practice and application. Yet others said it was more or less than 10,000 hours.

There's probably not one hard and fast rule that applies universally, yet the undeniable fact remains that gaining true Mastery in anything takes time, devotion, and applied effort no matter what it is you're trying to gain Mastery in or your base level of raw talent and natural gifts in that area.

And therein lies the rub as our modern-day culture is heavily skewed towards all that's fast, easy, and convenient. We want,

expect, and even demand Life to give us quick and easy riches, a pill or injection to fix our ailments or diseases, and we want a hard body without putting too much, if any, time and effort in.

This sort of "Easy Street" thinking is poisonous mental delusion as it sets us up for a showdown with the realities of Life itself which won't knee down to our fantasies and delusions.

If we wish to gain Mastery in anything, we must be willing to walk the path of the apprentice.

The path of the apprentice is to be humble and realistic where we are today and at the same time crystal clear on where we aspire to go.

The apprentice will make a plan to learn and grow, seek out the necessary schools, courses, workshops, mentors, and teachers to hone and elevate their craft, and they will devote their time and effort in earnest.

There's honor in choosing to be an apprentice or student and set the exalted objective to turn our mediocrity or incompetence in a

174

given area and turn it into an area of true Mastery.

The Conceit in Incompetence.

Conceit is rooted in arrogance, complacency, egotism, immodesty, vanity, false pride, and smugness.

The conceit in incompetence is not the incompetence or mediocrity itself, but the typical expectation we should be seen, regarded, respected (or compensated) for levels of Mastery we simply don't possess (yet).

This is simply our Egoic Mind at work as it will always gravitate towards resisting any notion we might not (yet) be very good at something—being humble just doesn't come natural to our Egoic Mind.

If you paid attention, I intentionally used the word "yet" twice already— because any level of incompetence or mediocrity is simply a temporary station and never a permanent condition.

Since we can know and embrace this tendency of our Egoic Mind, we can also easily neutralize this sort of thinking by reframing incompetence not to mean anything about us because that's usually where it really rubs for our Egoic Mind.

As a human being, we are each already whole and complete

regardless of what levels of incompetence or Mastery we might have in any given area.

Gaining Mastery in any area—even such things as love relationships or parenthood—doesn't make us a more worthy or valuable human being. All it does and can do is enrich our ability to enhance and deepen our experience of Life itself.

The very opening to step into the humbleness of apprenticeship is within internalizing this nuance— remind yourself often you are already perfectly imperfect, whole, and complete.

Finally, the general litmus test is that we're on our way to true Mastery not when we believe we are, but when others start to recognize our Mastery—literally, the Outer World will mirror this back to you and when it does you can trust you've made big leaps and you can use this as fuel to keep deepening your Mastery as that journey has no final destination.

The Blueprint of Genius.

The most common misplaced presumption is that to realize our unique genius we need to be a prodigy of some sort.

What naturally flows from this false belief is that when we don't see ourselves as a prodigy with some inborn gift, we automatically conclude any sort of level of genius is not available to us. This line of thinking is only amplified if we tend to compare ourselves to others.

The blueprint of genius is unique to each individual and we are truly never in competition with anyone else. Nobody can do you as well as you can—so, none of us have any true competition as long as we stay in our own lane which is expressing the most authentic version of ourselves unto the canvas of all of Creation.

Furthermore, each one of us has unique dreams, wishes, and desires and those seeds are planted within our Heart for us to bring them into a lived experience—not just for ourselves but for the entire Universe to be beautified and enhanced.

Since the design of this entire Universe is premised on intelligence and perfection, each one of us is endowed with all the gifts, talents, superpowers, and access to the resources we'll need to manifest our deepest held dreams and desires into existence.

These gifts, talents, and superpowers might be dormant or still asleep, but all that means is we're invited to go on the journey of gaining Mastery and bring them to full blossom. In this way, we each have our unique genius—zero

exceptions—and the level of genius we might have compared to others is of no significance whatsoever as we can know we have the level of genius we need to manifest our dreams and desires.

So, rest assured that you have genius within you in those areas that are relevant to your journey of Life and what your Soul wants to bring into existence as a lived experience.

The Magnetism of Mastery.

Mastery, once realized, has an enormous magnetism to it as all sorts of favorable serendipities, circumstances, and people are naturally drawn closer through true Mastery.

This is because on a deep level the Universe and people recognize the journey it took for your gifts and talents to be perfected to the level of Mastery.

We all know true Mastery is rare and what's deemed scarce is inherently valuable. This is what makes Mastery such a potent "door opener" as quite literally new worlds open up to us once we've made the arduous journey from apprenticeship to Mastery.

Finally, the journey of gaining Mastery or "means" is the end as it's the journey that shapes and molds us, not the final destination.

176

KEY LESSON

QUALITY OF BEING

Mastery

POISON

Incompetence

ANTIDOTE

Genius

ACTION

1) Mastery is a decision

Are you ready, willing, and able to make a firm decision to commit yourself to "I Am Genius"?

☐ **Yes, I commit wholeheartedly.**

☐ **No, I am not ready.**

2) Get clear about your "Why"

From the perspective of self-love, write a brief note from you to you "why" your answer above is true for you in this moment—your "why" is what will motivate and drive you to take aligned action.

Note: "No" is also a perfectly valid answer if that what's true for you right now.

_____

_____

_____

_____

_____

_____

_____

_____

_____

_____

_____

LOVE+ TRUTH | dōjō

JOURNAL + NOTES

Key chapter takeaways

My growth opportunities – "the Gaps"

My next level aspiration - "the What"

_____

_____

_____

My next level do's - "the How"

_____

_____

_____

_____

_____

_____

_____

_____

Notes

_____

_____

_____

_____

_____

_____

_____

LOVE+ TRUTH. | dōjō

LIVE/VIDEO LESSON

CHAPTER

COMPLETION

THE JOURNEY FROM
Defeatism to Endurance

"ADVERSITY HAS THE EFFECT OF ELICITING TALENTS, WHICH IN PROSPEROUS CIRCUMSTANCES WOULD HAVE LAIN DORMANT."

- Heraclitus -

MACRO PRINCIPLE

"

Seedlings bear no fruit.

———

We can get destroyed by circumstances or others, but we can only be defeated by ourselves.

———

All sorts of rewards come to those who finish what they started.

TEACHING

But Did You Finish?

The highest quality "failure" is the one where we have taken it all the way to and over the finish line and then we conclude it didn't yield what we had hoped or aimed for.

If you start a marathon but don't finish it, you'll never know your time or experience the exhilaration of demonstrating to yourself that you were able to finish the race.

Of course, "failure" is never truly a failure as we can still learn from it so even "failure" is a win. But, the only tool we have to explain concepts is language so within the limitations of words I am using the word "failure" above.

What I am pointing at is often times the Outer World is never at fault or cause when we're defeated as we can only defeat ourselves.

We can get destroyed, humbled, discouraged, smashed, broken, devastated, and demolished by the circumstances in our Outer World but being defeated is exclusively an Inner World job. When we give up we're making the decision to be

defeated. Now, not all defeats are created equal—some serve us and some don't and the only way to know the difference is the wisdom of discernment (more on that later).

What kills most dreams and desires is not that we can't realize them, but the belief we can't realize them.

There are two surefire ways to not realize your dreams and desires: (a) never start; or (b) never finish.

There are many other reasons in between that might (temporarily) derail, stunt, or slow you down but these two are the most important ones to bear in Mind.

For this chapter, we're going to assume we started as Completion doesn't even come into play unless we started.

The Malice of Defeatism.

Defeatism is a form of hopelessness or the mental state where we can't see our way out anymore and out of this hopelessness, capitulating starts accumulating a gravitational pull which eventually has us throw

186

in the towel. Let's unpack this a bit more as defeatism is at the root of not realizing Completion and without Completion we never get to harvest the fruits of the seeds we planted.

Within defeatism—which is mental in nature—there are two errors that can creep into our thinking which probably make up 80% of all giving up prematurely which is to say before we reach Completion.

The first principal error is the erroneous belief it should be easy, smooth, or convenient.

Just because you're on the right path, doesn't necessarily mean this path is always going to easy, smooth, and convenient. Often times, it's simply not as you're likely stretching and growing as you embark on this journey of creating and realizing a lived experience you haven't experienced before.

Any time we venture into the unknown—the uncharted path for us—we're going to have to learn, grow, and evolve into a higher version of ourselves so we become "that" version of ourselves which can have this previously unattainable lived experience (whatever that might be).

Hence, you can almost be assured it will not be easy, smooth, and convenient and yet many interpret

the resistance they're encountering as a sign they're not on the right path. Resistance, of course, is exclusively due to our perception of the circumstances and never the circumstances themselves.

The circumstances are always neutral—they are just "what is"—it's our perception that creates the story or narrative what we belief they are.

Two people faced with identical circumstances will likely have very different perceptions—and based on these perceptions they will each respond very differently.

In the metaphor again of running a marathon, the belief the whole race should be easy, smooth, and convenient (e.g. because you trained so hard) sets you up for defeatism when you then encounter some inevitable "challenge" during the race.

Conversely, going into the race knowing it's normal for every racer to encounter a challenge along the way but also feeling confident you have what it takes to overcome the challenge when it shows up will set you up for being able to "endure" the rough patch if/when it shows up —incidentally, this mindset of endurance is such a powerful state that what would have been perceived as a challenge doesn't even register at the level of a real challenge anymore. This is the power of our perception and its ability to reframe everything wherein the "thing" is only what we perceive it to be, not what it objectively is.

The second principal error is to succumb to time travel.

Most successful entrepreneurs will tell you if they knew upfront how difficult it was going to be, they would have likely never started.

Mountaineers and climbers know that midway the ascend to the summit, thinking about the whole climb still ahead is demoralizing and usually leads to a deflation of spirits where the climb inevitably becomes undoable.

Again, in the metaphor of running a marathon, once the race is well underway, the seasoned runner knows to only worry about the next mile marker or even the next 1-2 min to run—allowing the Mind to dwell on the whole remaining race is counterproductive and often times leads to defeatism creeping in and when it does the actual race is no longer the obstacle, the negative mental loops are. Often, this is where the runner is then defeated.

The point is this, once you've started you're focus and energy should be devoted to the next best step, move, or action you can take. You don't need to forget where you're going, but time travel will render the road ahead so long and arduous you'll likely defeat yourself before you can get to Completion.

The Essence of Endurance.

Cultivating the quality of endurance is what gets you to Completion and only within Completion, you get to harvest the fruits for the seeds you sowed.

Importantly, this also holds true for such things as love relationships and marriages.

Any couple that has been in a long-term relationship which is still mutually enriching and beautifully alive will tell you there were rough patches and dry spells. There were times when things weren't so great and all wasn't sunshine and roses.

But, these couples endured these lesser times as they invariably held on to a vision of what the relationship could be and so they persevered and got to the other side of the rough patch where they got to harvest the fruits of an even deeper love.

There's an element of wisdom and discernment in what needs to be completed and seen through; yet, that decision should never come from defeatism—this is why the quality of endurance is so vital.

188

KEY LESSON

QUALITY OF BEING

Completion

POISON

Defeatism

ANTIDOTE

Endurance

ACTION

1) Completion is a decision

Are you ready, willing, and able to make a firm decision to commit yourself to "I Am Enduring"?

☐ **Yes, I commit wholeheartedly.**

☐ **No, I am not ready.**

2) Get clear about your "Why"

From the perspective of self-love, write a brief note from you to you "why" your answer above is true for you in this moment—your "why" is what will motivate and drive you to take aligned action.

Note: "No" is also a perfectly valid answer if that what's true for you right now.

_____

_____

_____

_____

_____

_____

_____

_____

_____

_____

_____

LOVE+TRUTH | dōjō

JOURNAL + NOTES

Key chapter takeaways

My growth opportunities - "the Gaps"

My next level aspiration - "the What"

_____

_____

_____

My next level do's - "the How"

_____

_____

_____

_____

_____

_____

_____

_____

Notes

_____

_____

_____

_____

_____

_____

_____

_____

LOVE+ TRUTH | dōjō

LIVE/VIDEO LESSON

CHAPTER

SHOSHIN

THE JOURNEY FROM
False Pride to Receptiveness

"IT'S IMPOSSIBLE FOR A MAN TO LEARN WHAT HE THINKS HE ALREADY KNOWS."

- Epictetus -

196

MACRO PRINCIPLE

66

Your biggest foes are conceit and vanity.

———————

We cannot learn what we think we already know.

———————

Knowing & embracing the imposters is to no longer be fooled by them.

TEACHING

Survival Mechanisms.

Our Egoic Mind's principal objective —before anything else—is to ensure our safety, protection, and survival.

It's designed this way for good reason as we must survive or the game is over here on the Earthly realm, at least for this round.

The "problem" is the Egoic Mind makes no real distinction between physical and psychological survival —it's all the same to our Egoic Mind, survival is survival.

This inherent dilemma is where the phenomenon of false pride originates—it's a defense mechanism for the Egoic Mind much like a puffer fish makes itself look larger than it actually is when it feels threatened.

False pride comes in all sorts of gradations and varieties such as self-aggrandizing, arrogance, bragging, boasting, or grandiosity but it's not so much the outer appearance that matters most.

False pride is a distortion of the Ego in how it views itself, and it does so to deflect from something that it

simply doesn't want to see. At the core of this is typically some variation of low self-esteem, self-worth, self-love, or simply not being good enough (in the perception of the Egoic Mind).

False pride is what covers over these deeper wounds with a thin veneer of all the expressions referenced before—in this way it blinds us from not only these deeper wounds, but our lens gets really foggy in our ability to observe the world as it is and see ourselves in a true light.

Moreover, it closes us off from learning, growing, and evolving as this false pride acts like a shield or moat as we're too fragile to embrace there are areas where we're still just an apprentice.

As the wise quote of the Stoic philosopher Epictetus mentioned before: "A man cannot learn what he thinks he already knows."

The Reward of Receptiveness.

The quality of Being we're after in this chapter is "Shoshin" which is a Buddhist teaching of always having a "beginner's mind" in all situations and circumstances. This teaching is profound in that if we can withhold our perceptions—which are inherently just our relative or subjective Truth—then we have an opportunity to be with what truly is.

The pathway to Shoshin is cultivating receptiveness which is an openness of Mind free of what we think we know already.

The Truth is, we know very little in general and we think we know a lot —this is the natural consequence of our Mind being a meaning-making machine.

As of our first breath, our Mind starts processing all sensory inputs and starts giving everything a meaning. The cumulative build-up of this web of meaning of everything that has ever occurred to us creates in our subconscious mind an understanding—a library of sorts—of our reality and Life itself.

Our lens of our perception of whatever might occur in our Life is always colored by the coloration of this library our subconscious mind has created from all our experiences during this lifetime.

Our early childhood years up to around age 7-8 are especially formative as our Mind is predominantly in Theta brainwaves during these years which allows the Mind to be a sponge of information.

This explains why young children can learn language—multiple languages even—so easily and why they are so receptive in general to learning new skills, behaviors, habits, and patterns.

They are literally very moldable as we are each born with our Mind in Shoshin mode.

As our sense of small self (i.e. Ego) comes online and develops, and we start to adopt the social, cultural, and religious values that we are taught through our upbringing, early school years, and external influences like TV shows we slowly but surely start to form a basic framework of our reality based on all these inputs.

By around age 7-8, our Mind then switches to be predominantly in Beta and Alpha brainwave states which is where our Mind will operate the rest of our Life. Practices like meditation can still give us access to the Theta state, but it's no longer our daily waking state.

Within the Beta and Alpha brainwave state, we can still have high levels of receptiveness but that can only come through our awareness and bringing receptiveness to the forefront in our conscious mind. Basically, we have to cultivate the ability to overwrite the autopilot function of the Mind which is to have the subconscious mind process, interpret, and assign meaning to whatever floods in through our five senses.

Receptiveness then is an active application of our awareness to disregard preconceived notions and automatic responses from the subconscious mind and direct our conscious mind to stay open.

We truly step into becoming the Observer and we keep our conscious mind as a blank movie screen so it can receive the film of our reality flooding in through our five senses in its purest reflection.

Just imagine projecting a film on a movie screen that is not blank—this would distort the film being projected on the movie screen as whatever is already on the screen will interfere with what's actually on the film.

Whatever we hold in our subconscious mind as our beliefs and understanding of ourselves, our reality, and Life itself is basically always playing interference with the "neutral data" that's flooding in through our five senses—we don't truly see our experiences for what they are, we see them in how we perceive them to be.

Receptiveness is the ability to keep our movie screen as blank as

humanly possible so we can be open to what truly is.

Since receptiveness is correlated with our level of awareness, all of this is correlated directly with our level of consciousness—the higher we ascend, the more access we regain (since we had it when we were born) to true Shoshin.

The Wisdom of Shoshin.

There's a reason Shoshin is so highly regarded in the Buddhist tradition as the Buddha himself stated: "The root cause of all pain and suffering is ignorance."

Ignorance is of course the lack of knowledge but that lack often stems from us simply "seeing" things in a distorted way due to the coloration of our lens of perception.

The quality of Shoshin reveals itself in being open to feedback, criticism, and new concepts or alternative perspectives.

We can still conclude our own conclusions, but if we lack the receptiveness to welcome in all the above we cannot truly say we came to any conclusion as we just held on to whatever we already thought to be true before.

To paraphrase the poet Marcel Proust: "The real voyage of discovery is not to visit new landscapes but to see with new eyes."

200

KEY LESSON

QUALITY OF BEING

Shoshin

POISON

False Pride

ANTIDOTE

Receptiveness

ACTION

1) Shoshin is a decision

Are you ready, willing, and able to make a firm decision to commit yourself to "I Am Receptive"?

☐ **Yes, I commit wholeheartedly.**

☐ **No, I am not ready.**

2) Get clear about your "Why"

From the perspective of self-love, write a brief note from you to you "why" your answer above is true for you in this moment—your "why" is what will motivate and drive you to take aligned action.

Note: "No" is also a perfectly valid answer if that what's true for you right now.

_____

_____

_____

_____

_____

_____

_____

_____

_____

_____

_____

LOVE+ TRUTH | dōjō

JOURNAL + NOTES

Key chapter takeaways

My growth opportunities - "the Gaps"

My next level aspiration - "the What"

_____

_____

_____

My next level do's - "the How"

_____

_____

_____

_____

_____

_____

_____

_____

Notes

_____

_____

_____

_____

_____

_____

_____

_____

LOVE+
TRUTH. | dōjō

LIVE/VIDEO LESSON

CHAPTER

GRATITUDE

THE JOURNEY FROM
Morosity to Vision

"WEAR GRATITUDE LIKE A CLOAK, AND IT WILL FEED EVERY CORNER OF YOUR LIFE."

- Rumi -

MACRO PRINCIPLE

"

Optimism changes the tapestry of reality.

No pessimist has ever scaled new peaks or discovered new lands.

Optimism is the on-switch for Gratitude, pessimism is the off-button.

TEACHING

Seeing What You Look For.

What's likely coming through as an overarching message within these chapters is that Life itself is not necessarily what it is but what we perceive it to be.

Nothing could be more true for Gratitude which is, as a vibration and frequency, an unequalled manifestation amplifier.

Gratitude has everything to do with how we choose to perceive our Life and its ever-changing facts and circumstances—in that way, Gratitude is a lens through which we choose to see Life and that's what literally changes everything while nothing might be any different factually.

Morosity is the state of being morose which is to say sullen, gloomy, sad, glum, or depressed— in this state we simply have no "eyes" for any of the blessings or good things in our Life.

When we're morose, everything in our Life gets covered with a thick layer of muck. It holds a very low vibration and it drains our energy

so we tend to become lethargic, apathetic, and sluggish. As we're down on ourselves and Life, we tend to seek our solace in escapism such as drinking alcohol, smoking weed, binge-watching TV or gambling. We become vulnerable to addictions to all sorts of narcotic substances including prescription anti-depressants or sleeping aids.

The downward spiral is real, and we can get stuck here for a long time as our society (and the System) is highly accepting of functional escapees and addicts—not just accepting, in many cases we think it's normal.

In the profound words of Jiddu Krisnamurti: "It's no measure of health to be well-adjusted to a profoundly sick society."

From just the narrow perspective of manifestation, the greatest problem with morosity—besides the low vibration and frequency— is that it shuts down our vision altogether.

Coincidences, serendipities, and all the other sorts of magic that comes to our aid daily doesn't stop when we're morose, we just can't see or

210

recognize them anymore. We quite literally lose our vision for them when we're in a prolonged funk or when pessimism becomes our general outlook on Life.

Pessimism has a way of obscuring all that's good, beautiful, and miraculous in our Life; whereas, optimism has a way of revealing it.

The early onset and tell-tale sign that morosity is starting to infiltrate your Being is complaining. Complaining is also an energy drain but even more so what we resist will always persist. Complaining feeds and funnels energy into something we don't like (or worse) and thereby keeps it alive.

We all know this as nothing has ever gone away by complaining about it. Things naturally dissipate and dissolve when we stop giving it mental airtime and energy or, in other words, when we stop thinking about it.

Visionary Vision.

With Gratitude, we're not just looking to cultivate ordinary vision, we are actually looking for a very specific flavor of vision I refer to as "visionary vision."

Visionary implies "that" which is right beyond the horizon of ordinary sight, perhaps even a little further for others as what's already real and apparent for the visionary is typically entirely out of sight for others.

Now, before we go deeper into this visionary vision, I want to make sure I don't dismiss the value and importance of ordinary vision.

Having and cultivating vision for all the good, beautiful, and miraculous in our Life is a prerequisite for Gratitude and in addition a pivotal steppingstone to leaning into our visionary vision.

So, with the presumption that we have an optimistic disposition on Life itself and our ordinary vision is running on all cylinders at least most of the time, we can explore what's so special and unique about visionary vision.

As explained, with visionary vision we're pointing at being able to see beyond the horizon for the attractions to come. These attractions of course are those dreams, wishes, and desires we have chosen we want to manifest into our Life as a lived experience.

Albert Einstein said: "Imagination is everything. It is the preview of life's coming attractions."

Those words by one of the 20th century's most brilliant physicists could have come from a guru, sage, or mystic and, personally, I actually believe Einstein was as much a spiritual prodigy as he was a genius physicist.

Let me unpack why.

Everything starts with imagination—it's the origin point where we give shape and form to the unmanifest. First as a mere idea or concept which then can be transmuted into manifest form.

Without imagination, there's nothing to manifest into form or matter or a lived experience as this Universe is just an infinite plenum (vs a void or vaccum) which holds infinite yet undefined potentialities.

Imagination—in the form of an idea, dream, or desire—is "that" which lies just beyond the horizon of our ordinary sight. We can't quite see it yet as it's not yet manifest, but we can feel and connect with it as it becomes ever-more "real" to us in our imagination.

The process of manifesting anything from the unmanifest spiritual or metaphysical realm to the manifest material or physical realm takes energy—quite a bit of energy as what starts as an ethereal imagination has to be transformed into something that has accumulated sufficient energy to become materialized in our objective reality as a lived

experience. The way we feed anything energy in our imagination is to live and experience it in imagination as if it's already fulfilled in our reality—and that's the very essence of visionary vision.

Visionary vision is seeing, living, feeling, and experiencing that which is not yet manifest to such a degree that your Mind can't tell the difference anymore—to your Mind it's as if you already have it.

The Power of Gratitude.

To have Gratitude for something you're not sure you can or will have is next to impossible.

On the contrary, it's quite easy to have Gratitude for something that you experience as something you already have, even though the objective manifest experience is not quite here yet.

This sort of Gratitude is like putting rocket fuel in your manifesting engine as the vibration and frequency of Gratitude is extraordinarily high.

High frequency corresponds with high energy so all other things being equal, Gratitude adds an enormous infusion of energy and as we described before energy is what's needed to transmute the unmanifest into the manifest. In fact, next to Love, Gratitude is the magical pixie dust of this Universe.

212

KEY LESSON

QUALITY OF BEING
Gratitude

POISON
Morosity

ANTIDOTE
Vision

ACTION

1) Gratitude is a decision

Are you ready, willing, and able to make a firm decision to commit yourself to "I Am Visionary"?

☐ **Yes, I commit wholeheartedly.**

☐ **No, I am not ready.**

2) Get clear about your "Why"

From the perspective of self-love, write a brief note from you to you "why" your answer above is true for you in this moment—your "why" is what will motivate and drive you to take aligned action.

Note: "No" is also a perfectly valid answer if that what's true for you right now.

_____

_____

_____

_____

_____

_____

_____

_____

_____

_____

LOVE+ TRUTH | dōjō

JOURNAL + NOTES

Key chapter takeaways

My growth opportunities - "the Gaps"

My next level aspiration - "the What"

_____

_____

_____

My next level do's - "the How"

_____

_____

_____

_____

_____

_____

_____

_____

Notes

_____

_____

_____

_____

_____

_____

_____

LOVE+ TRUTH. | dōjō

LIVE/VIDEO LESSON

CHAPTER

Bonus

TEMPERANCE

THE JOURNEY FROM
Gluttony to Magnanimity

LOVE+TRUTH | dōjō

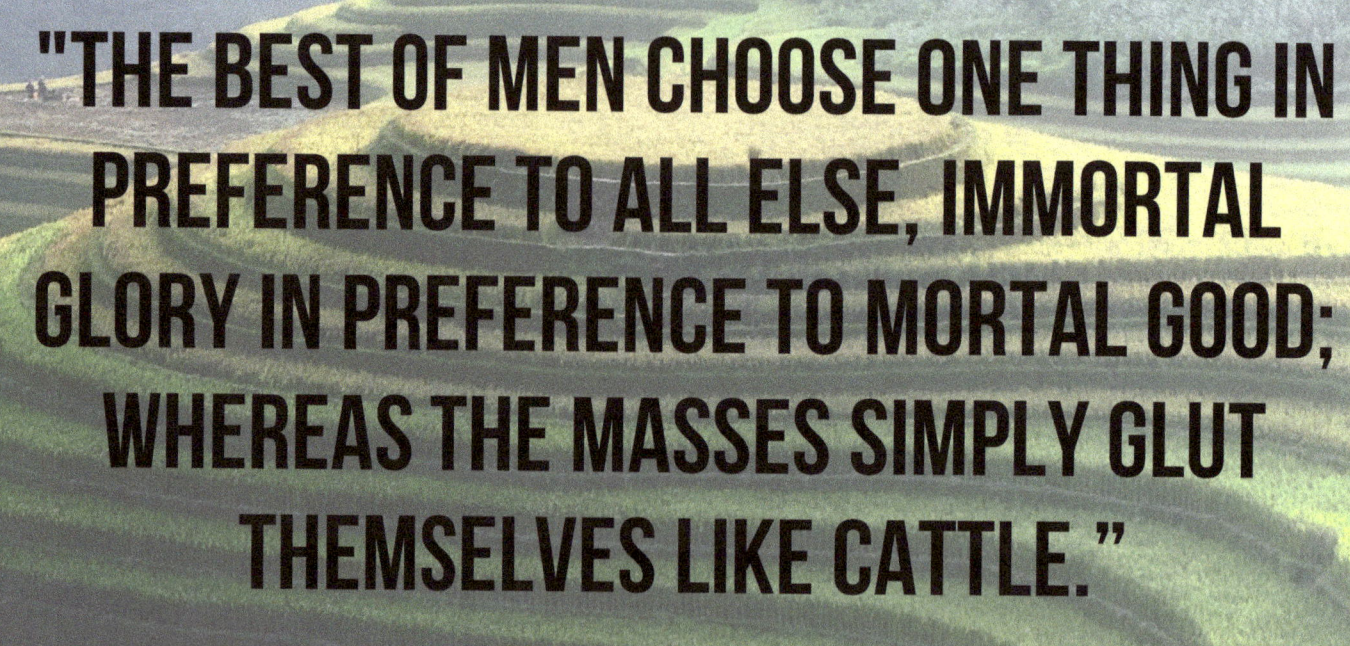

"THE BEST OF MEN CHOOSE ONE THING IN PREFERENCE TO ALL ELSE, IMMORTAL GLORY IN PREFERENCE TO MORTAL GOOD; WHEREAS THE MASSES SIMPLY GLUT THEMSELVES LIKE CATTLE."

- Heraclitus -

MACRO PRINCIPLE

"

The sweetest fruit takes time to ripen.

———

Life itself is never in a rush, we tend to be impatient and want things sooner.

———

Yet, knowing when it's time to harvest yields the richest crops.

TEACHING

Who Owns Who?

Within Temperance, the question is whether our desires and cravings own us, or if we own them.

Temperance is a very big topic as our ability to be the master of our cravings and delay gratification is a leading indicator of how successful we'll be in the material realm by the measures of this realm.

There's no need for any judgment in the way success is measured in the material realm, there's nothing inherently wrong with trophies, fame, fortune, and applause provided we know that the "game Man plays" is a Finite Game that plays out at all times within the "game Spirit plays" which is the eternal Infinite Game.

We run into challenges when we (a) don't realize the game Man plays is within the game Spirit plays; or (b) we get lost in either the game Man plays or the game Spirit plays for that matter.

Let's delve deeper in each of these —the first occurs when we're still unawakened from the dream of Life

or, as I sometimes refer to it, the truth serum hasn't dropped yet. The vast majority of the collective of humanity is still in this state, even though the rate of awakening is accelerating in meaningful ways.

Nevertheless, none of us can consciously choose or elect for the truth serum to be dropped—this happens when it happens by the invisible hand of a Higher Order in perfect timing for our evolutionary journey. A person is not better, more worthy, or more advanced for having awakened so we can just embrace we're each at different places and all is in perfect order.

What we can know is that for those that have not yet awakened, the game Spirit plays simply doesn't exist and cannot be known so, naturally, all that exists for them in their experience of reality is the game Man plays.

For some, the absence of the awareness and understanding of the game Spirit plays makes no difference on how they "play" the game Man plays—they are naturally innocent at Heart and will not degrade into greed, fraud, crimes,

222

malfeasance, dishonesty, etc. to "win" in the game Man plays. Yet (unawakened) others do degrade into all these shadow aspects we each have within. They are not really lost in the game Man plays though, as all they are aware of is the game Man plays—they are at a loss of their innocence which can only happen when that's within their lesson plan for this lifetime.

We each have our own lesson plan, and the objective is to stick to our own plan and reject the temptation to judge others.

The second challenge can only occur when we have awakened from the dream of Life, even if that is still very fresh and in the preliminary stages of awakening.

By definition, it's only when we have awakened that we can get lost in either the game Man plays or the game Spirit plays—and, either way, we're lost so one is no better or worse than the other.

The purpose of incarnating in a human avatar here in Earth school is to integrate, harmonize, and master these two distinct games which play out simultaneously in different dimensions of reality.

To get lost in the game Man plays is to lose sight of our spiritual essence; conversely, to get lost in the game Spirit plays is to lose sight

of our physical or carnal nature which is called "spiritual bypassing" in colloquial terms.

With that foundational framework in place, let's now delve into Temperance starting with the poison called gluttony.

The Toxin called Gluttony.

The dictionary defines gluttony as a ravenous craving, hunger, lust, thirst, greed, and hankering.

Just within that we can clearly see how gluttony is beyond the satisfaction of a normal healthy appetite as it crosses into overindulgence and excess beyond what we truly need.

The toxic nature of gluttony is that as the things desired become a craving, the things now come to own us.

We can see this play out on many levels wherever and whenever we cross into excess whether that's food, alcohol, drugs, partying, gambling, consumerism, sex, etc.

We see this in the enormous amounts of consumer goods and especially frivolous luxury items purchased with debt or credit cards which implies in reality these consumers are purchasing goods and services they can't really afford. When we become beholden to having to have things "now" that we in reality can't afford or don't truly need, we have fallen victim to our own gluttony.

Gluttony enslaves us to the System and its seductive lure that "things" in the Outer World can pacify our true Inner World desires—they can't, all gluttony can do is get you stuck on that hamster wheel.

In the words of Epictetus: "Wealth consists not in having great possessions, but in having few wants."

The point here is not in how much we have materially—as that might be a lot or very little as the case might be and neither of those is inherently good nor bad, right nor wrong—the point is to have few wants regardless of what we have as therein lies our mastery of Temperance.

Our Magnanimous Nature.

Magnanimous was a term first coined by the Greek philosopher Aristotle where "magna" stands for great and "animous" stands for Soul. Aristotle used this word to express the concept of a person having mastered the virtue of being great of Mind and Heart—another way to paraphrase this is to say a person that has realized his/her true nature of his/her highest potential.

Aristotle and the school of Greek philosophy held a core belief that each person—each Soul—is magnanimous in essence. We each hold all powers, wisdom, and potential within which in Buddhist traditions is called our Buddha nature and is also referred to as the Christos within each of us or Christ Consciousness.

The virtue of Temperance is a quality of Being recognized in every ancient wisdom traditions as an important pathway to realizing our full potential as we rise above the temptations of gluttony and overindulgence which are all cravings of our lower carnal nature.

The Wealth of Temperance.

When we become the master of our cravings and master the delay of gratification we move into a distinctly higher dimension of our manifestation powers.

Temperance is this pathway, and this has nothing to do with having to live like a monk or reject material possessions or even wealth.

We can fully engage with the material realm and enjoy all the riches and carnal fruits it has to offer provided we don't become owned by our lust and cravings for the "things" of the Outer World.

In the end, Temperance is a reflection of our magnanimity— being truly great of Mind and Heart.

224

KEY LESSON

QUALITY OF BEING

Temperance

POISON

Gluttony

ANTIDOTE

Magnanimity

ACTION

1) Temperance is a decision

Are you ready, willing, and able to make a firm decision to commit yourself to "I Am Magnanimous"?

☐ **Yes, I commit wholeheartedly.**

☐ **No, I am not ready.**

2) Get clear about your "Why"

From the perspective of self-love, write a brief note from you to you "why" your answer above is true for you in this moment—your "why" is what will motivate and drive you to take aligned action.

Note: "No" is also a perfectly valid answer if that what's true for you right now.

_____

_____

_____

_____

_____

_____

_____

_____

_____

_____

_____

LOVE+ TRUTH. | dōjō

JOURNAL + NOTES

Key chapter takeaways

My growth opportunities - "the Gaps"

My next level aspiration - "the What"

_____

_____

_____

My next level do's - "the How"

_____

_____

_____

_____

_____

_____

_____

_____

Notes

_____

_____

_____

_____

_____

_____

_____

_____

LOVE+
TRUTH | dōjō

LIVE/VIDEO LESSON

About Robert

**LOVE+
TRUTH**

KNOW THYSELF

THE GRAND ODYSSEY: MASTERY OF LIFE ITSELF

Robert Althuis is the author of the Amazon bestsellers "Love+Truth" and "Never Enoughitis" and the Founder of the Sacred Wealth Collective, a mindfulness organization that provides coaching, strategies, tools, and techniques to help private clients and businesses embody their full human potential.

Robert is a sought-after spiritual mentor, keynote speaker, regenerative capitalism advisor, and regenerative real estate entrepreneur.

He resides in Miami, Florida and is a father, artist, yogi (RYT-200), kite surfer, crossfit athlete, and an active dive volunteer with the Coral Restoration Foundation in the Florida Keys where he previously served as a Board Member.

Credentials

Current Business Engagements:

- Founder - Love & Truth PB LLC
- Founder - Wayfare Impact LLC
- Chief Change Agent - NewStar Media
- Advisory Board Member - Bulltick - Domum Fund I & II

Prior Business Engagements:

Robert launched Wayfare in early 2009 with the acquisition of a 50% ownership position in Lynxs, a leading international transportation infrastructure development firm based in Austin, Texas. Prior to acquiring an ownership position in Lynxs, Mr. Althuis was a Senior Vice President in the Airport Infrastructure group of GE Capital Aviation Services (GECAS). At GECAS, Mr. Althuis served as the lead originator for the Americas Region of the Airport Infrastructure group and was instrumental in structuring Global Infrastructure Partners, a then $10 billion infrastructure investment fund sponsored by GE and Credit Suisse as well as the acquisition of numerous operating companies and real assets on behalf of GECAS where he also served as board member on behalf of GE. Mr. Althuis started his career at GE Capital in an executive management program in 2002 and joined GECAS on a full-time basis in 2003 and was promoted to GE's executive band (top 1% of GE) in 2006. In his initial role in GECAS, as a member of the structured finance team, Mr. Althuis closed in excess of $1.5 billion of aviation related debt and equity financings.

Mr. Althuis started his career in real estate in 1995 in Atlanta, GA where he joined a regional development and investment firm which he left as a Partner & Senior Vice President in '01 to attend Columbia Businesss School in NYC.

Academic Credentials:

- Columbia Business School New York, NY - MBA with distinction with a major in Finance & Management
- Georgia State University Atlanta, GA - BBA summa cum laude with a major in Real Estate
- University of Amsterdam Amsterdam, The Netherlands - Associates Degree in Political Science
- Hogeschool van Amsterdam Amsterdam, The Netherlands - Associates Degree in Economics

Professional Credentials:

- Licensed Real Estate Broker in the state of Florida (GA & TX inactive)
- Licensed General Contractor in the state of Florida (inactive)
- Certified Member of the CCIM Institute (inactive)
- Certified Coaching Facilitator
- Certified Six Sigma Black Belt (GE Crotonville)
- Graduate of GE's Management Development Curriculum (MDC)
- Certified Yoga Instructor (RYT200)
- Certified Medium - Delphi University
- Former U.S. Professional Tennis Association Certified Professional

233

LOVE+
TRUTH™

ISBN # 979-8-218-48052-3